W9-AVB-696

LIFESTYLE ENTREPRENEUR

Praise for
LIFESTYLE ENTREPRENEUR

Krieger carries you over the most important threshold in an entrepreneur's life: From "I can't" to "I can". If you want to be one of the ones that "can", read this book!
—**Bryan Franklin**, Co-Creator of Mind Money Meaning

In Lifestyle Entrepreneur, Jesse Krieger gives a realistic, down-to-earth approach on creating business ventures from the road. This book includes productive tips that make the unimaginable possible. A great tool for aspiring **entrepreneurs.**
—**Alicia Dunams**, Bestselling Author and Creator of BestsellerInAWeekend.com

I've made more money in 2 months than working the last 6 at my previous corporate job. Now I travel the world building a network of friends and business contacts that is well beyond what I previously imagined possible. Reading Lifestyle Entrepreneur and joining Jesse Krieger's mentorship and community has been one of the smartest investment I've made in a long time.
—**Myke Macapinlac**, Author of *Magnetic Dating* and a proud Lifestyle Entrepreneur.

I love the idea of identifying your interests to discover your identity. I have already subconsciously done this but hadn't ever taken such an analytical approach to it. Previously, if you asked me what I wanted most in life, I might have just answered with a cliché "to be happy." But Lifestyle Entrepreneur supplies a great construct for figuring out what it takes to truly be happy and how to create that lifestyle for myself.
—**Amber Gibson**, Freelance Food & Travel Writer

Thank you so much for sharing your knowledge and experience in this book! In the past I started two online businesses that failed, but using techniques described in Lifestyle Entrepreneur, along with the exercises provided, I have now setup my own business that compliments my life and interest. A must read for all aspiring entrepreneurs!
—**Matty Davis**, Founder of Stubby Holder Wholesaler, Australia

Lifestyle Entrepreneur gave me a life-changing idea. I realized that I have been doing things that I truly don't want to do, and now I'm committed to combining all the things I love and serving others through my business. I am making big changes in my life because of this book. Thank you so much!

—**Pekka Mattila**, Co-Founder of Intoloop, Finland

I cannot recommend Lifestyle Entrepreneur and working with Jesse enough. The skills he teaches and the life he leads are the tools and motivation that will allow you to take your life to the next level!

—**Davin Piercey**, PhD in Explosives Chemistry and entrepreneur

This book is a must for anyone wanting success while enjoying the things they are passionate about in life. I actually read the whole book in one night and my only regret is that I didn't discover Lifestyle Entrepreneur sooner.

—**Brandon Pinney**, Former Sales Manager turned entrepreneur

If you are looking to turn your passions into profits, even if you have no business experience and just want to take control of your life, Jesse Krieger is the man who can help you. He'll save you money on costs and tell you how it is for any of your ideas.

—**Dan Dynneson**, Canadian engineer turned entrepreneur

After devouring Lifestyle Entrepreneur in under 24 hours, I got straight to work restructuring my SEO business to support my ideal lifestyle based on Jesse's suggestions. Now I can soon fulfill my dream of living abroad in Thailand for a year, where I want to take my passion for Muay Thai kickboxing to a whole new level. I can hear the crack of shins against a heavy bag already!

—**Chris Grimm**, SEO expert and entrepreneur

Lifestyle Entrepreneur is a fantastic book! It begins by helping you find what you're truly passionate about in life, and then cultivates those passions into something that you can utilize as a business venture. Jesse walks you through every step from concept to implementation using exercises, theory and personal experiences.

—**Cole Sekedat**, Student at Western Washington University

Reading Lifestyle Entrepreneur made me reconsider the path my life is on. After traveling around Asia for a few months looking for inspiration, the idea struck and now I'm building a business that incorporates my love of travel and rock climbing and couldn't be more excited. Thanks for the inspiration!

—**Manuel Kraemer**, St. Gallen University, Switzerland

LIFESTYLE ENTREPRENEUR

**Live Your Dreams,
Ignite Your Passions and
Run Your Business From Anywhere In The World**

JESSE KRIEGER

NEW YORK

LIFESTYLE ENTREPRENEUR

Live Your Dreams, Ignite Your Passions and Run Your Business From Anywhere In The World

© 2014 **Jesse Krieger**.

All rights reserved. No portion of this book may be reproduced, stored in a retrieval system, or transmitted in any form or by any means—electronic, mechanical, photocopy, recording, scanning, or other,—except for brief quotations in critical reviews or articles, without the prior written permission of the publisher.

Published in New York, New York, by Morgan James Publishing. Morgan James and The Entrepreneurial Publisher are trademarks of Morgan James, LLC. www.MorganJamesPublishing.com

The Morgan James Speakers Group can bring authors to your live event. For more information or to book an event visit The Morgan James Speakers Group at www.TheMorganJamesSpeakersGroup.com.

FREE eBook edition for your existing eReader with purchase

PRINT NAME ABOVE

For more information, instructions, restrictions, and to register your copy, go to **www.bitlit.ca/readers/register** or use your QR Reader to scan the barcode:

ISBN 978-1-61448-627-5 paperback
ISBN 978-1-61448-628-2 eBook
ISBN 978-1-61448-629-9 audio
ISBN 978-1-61448-901-6 hard cover
Library of Congress Control Number: 2013934261

Cover Design by:
Jesse Krieger
www.JesseKrieger.com

Interior Design by:
Bonnie Bushman
bonnie@caboodlegraphics.com

In an effort to support local communities, raise awareness and funds, Morgan James Publishing donates a percentage of all book sales for the life of each book to Habitat for Humanity Peninsula and Greater Williamsburg.

Get involved today, visit
www.MorganJamesBuilds.com

Habitat for Humanity®
Peninsula and Greater Williamsburg
Building Partner

ACKNOWLEDGEMENTS

To my family for always believing in me; Thanks to my father Ken, my mother Sue and sister Michelle.

To everyone I have started a business with, you inspire and teach me; Jake Harsh, Jamie Speirs, Tom Rubin, Mike Jackson, Robby Bearman, Elena Alexa, Rachel O'Reilly, Bryce Anderson, Todd Sipes, Dak Steiert.

To the mentors who have empowered my dreams, Michael Doyle, Paul Falchi, Ned Brokaw, Mitch Tuchman, Wayne Van Dyck, Alfred Mandel, Bob & Jill Hamer, Monte Lawrence, Abol Hosseinioun, and Joel Yanowitz.

To my awesome friends in the Project Rockstar crew around the world, let the good times roll, Jim Stark, Jeremy Bonney, Thompson Plyler, Daniel Vercetti, Nick Hoss, Andrew Smith, Andrew Yeoh, and all of you. Big shout out to Marcus Ho for believing in this book...and Shakil Khan for introducing me to China.

To my friends, classmates and teachers throughout the years, let us always embrace a culture of life-long learning.

This book is dedicated to You! That you may have satisfaction in this life.

And most of all, thanks to God who makes all things possible.

TABLE OF CONTENTS

FROM THE JUNGLES
OF BORNEO...

"I think this will make us better friends," Andrew said as we wove our way back into the crowded streets of Haadrin at 4:15 AM.

"Let's see how long we can make it before the typhoon rolls back in," I said side-stepping four loud Brits singing God Save The Queen with matching neon green headbands on.

"At least until sunrise, that's my bet,"he said as we both darted under the awning of a makeshift noodle restaurant to avoid the flatbed truck splashing through the alley with loudspeakers announcing Muay Thai fights the next night.

Moments later we arrived back at the beach, with the full moon staring us down, suspended over the mouth of the bay like a non-judgmental cyclops witnessing what was now only a few hundred people dancing and drinking to electro music pounding out of speaker stacks facing the waves.

The party is still going strong and despite almost calling it a night at 3:30, inspiration struck around 4:00 so we donned our sandals once more and rejoined the revelry. It's the final Full Moon Party of 2012 and I'm enjoying every minute of this mini-vacation from Malaysia where the *Lifestyle Entrepreneur* book tour is in full swing.

One week earlier I was celebrating Thanksgiving in Borneo, hiking through lush jungles with volcanic rock formations and the occasional family of foraging wild boars. And in between then and now I was on stages from Kuching, Sarawak to Kuala Lumpur, speaking at book fairs about *Lifestyle Entrepreneur* and meeting friends and fans along the way.

This trip was courtesy of Popular Books, the largest book chain in Malaysia, and Kanyin Publications, my Asian publisher. Two months after *Lifestyle Entrepreneur* came out in southeast Asia, the book hit #2 business best seller at Popular and from that came the opportunity to tour around the country all expenses paid.

Now it's 5:00 a.m. and the sky is turning a lighter shade of blue, but overhead clouds have gathered again and a few raindrops aren't stopping the throngs of locals and travelers dancing in the sand.

In the morning I'll grab a ferry back to Koh Samui and grab one last pad thai before catching a flight back to Kuala Lumpur. Then it's back on the tour circuit, driving through the lush Malaysian countryside to the Penang Mega Book Fair with my editor and a Kanyin sales executive sharing their favorite local foods at roadside markets along the way.

> **The feeling is profound to be hiking in the middle of the jungle one day, then on a stage presenting to a hundred people the next.**

If variety is the spice of life, then I like it hot. The feeling is profound to be hiking in the middle of the jungle one day, then on a stage presenting to a hundred people the next. To be planning book promotions over dim sum in a local market with my team, then catching a plane to Thailand to party with my friends and periodically working on our laptops in our tank tops.

While these events may seem disconnected, there is a common thread that runs between these extremes. The glue that ties these diverse experiences and adventures together is a passion for novelty, a deep interest in lifestyle design and a flare for entrepreneurship.

That's what pulls me forward and drives me to learn new industries and languages, to write a book or launch a business. I am pursuing my interest and passions, following them around the world, wherever they lead with a keen eye to how they can be turned into products and services that are valuable to others, that others will pay for in cash or in kind.

That's the path of a Lifestyle Entrepreneur and that's the road that lead me to this distant tropical island, dancing on the beach as the sun threatens to breach the horizon, just as the sky parts and a torrential downpour of rain pummels the beach. The sea of people parts and stream back towards their bungalows and hostels, leaving only the most dedicated to watch the sunrise as rainy season officially kicks off in the tropics.

Even though dancing in the rain on a tropical island at sunrise is the farthest thing from work I can think of, who knows, maybe I'll lead off my next book fair talk with this story. The ideas my friends and I shared over fresh seafood and Singhas could make my client's online business run way better, so when I jump on a video call with him in a few days, he'll be thrilled.

Separating the outcome from the experiential, these three days in Thailand make a damn good return on investment. But that's not really the way I look at it.

The way I see it, the world is both your playground and your potential addressable market. If you don't believe that, I'm going to do my best to convince you otherwise over the course of this book.

The world has changed over the last decade and technology has advanced to a point where it is entirely possible to build numerous businesses and run them all from a laptop, anywhere in the world. Online talent markets make it easy to hire and manage teams of designers and developers, while software that lives in the cloud can let you scale a business from hundreds of customers to hundreds of thousands without worrying about the technology.

This reality has dramatic implications; It no longer matters where you are.

I have processed invoices and managed a sales team from inside the Arctic Circle after watching the Northern Lights in Norway, and I have coached clients via video conference from Hong Kong after exploring ancient Buddhist temples around the island.

By setting up my businesses to run through the Internet, the only thing that matters is that I can access it from time to time. Where I am, who I'm with, and what I'm doing after I make my contribution doesn't factor into the equation.

> The way I see it, the world is both your playground and your potential addressable market.

What does matter is having a valuable product or service that others are willing to pay for, and the knowledge and experience to offer it in such a way that you are unconstrained by your geographic location.

That is what this book is all about!

Being a Lifestyle Entrepreneur is about pursuing your passions in creative and engaging ways and launching businesses that amplify your interests and support your ideal lifestyle. It's about learning what you need to know, to do the things you'd love to do, so you can ultimately be the person you aspire to be. It's about inspiring others through your acts, and instructing them through your experience.

Ultimately, it's about embracing a culture of life-long learning and living a life of distinction and making a positive impact on those you around you and of course having a lot of fun in the process!

Looking out at the world today, I see a time of tremendous change and opportunity.

Technology and innovation have brought down prices for computers, smart phones and tablets that let you carry more processing power in a backpack than fit in an entire room a few decades ago. The best universities make their best courses available for free online, allowing anyone with enough self-discipline to get a world-class education and shorten the learning curve to gain new skills. Social networks and software platforms let us stay in contact with friends and family as well as customers and suppliers all over the world.

> Being a Lifestyle Entrepreneur is about pursuing your passions in creative and engaging ways

OK, so I'm an optimist. But what about widening income inequality, chronic unemployment and lackluster economic growth in developed countries? Well, if there is any downside to all the exciting changes and opportunities taking place, it is that you need to be more versatile and adaptable than ever before.

Gone are the days of life-long employment with a blue chip firm. Gone are the days of looking at countries as a "closed economy" that is self-sufficient and can provide for itself with the power of its population alone. To me it's a foregone conclusion that the world is entirely interconnected and that opportunity doesn't recognize geopolitical boundaries.

The successful Lifestyle Entrepreneurs of today know all of this and put it into practice by traveling frequently for fun and financial motivations. Just in the last year alone, I took six international trips, more than half of which were fully paid for by others I was helping, working with or training.

I don't say that to brag, but rather to really show you what is possible when you put your mind to it. Here's a quick look at what my 2012 looked like:

After a family trip to Kauai just after New Years, I was flown to Hong Kong to co-instruct a dating workshop where my friend and co-instructor Thompson taught a group of guys how to have more success in their relationships and how to meet more women they are genuinely interested in.

Then in March I flew to Hong Kong to work on sourcing suppliers for a coaching client that built business selling wholesale drink coolers (or "stubby holders" as their called in Australia). After Hong Kong I continued on to Kuala Lumpur to finish negotiations with my Asian publisher. With a signed contract in hand, it was off to visit the surrounding jungles and Hindu temples in the Batu Caves before a quick stop in Singapore to visit friends on the way home.

After working on the book at home in San Francisco for a few months and coaching a few clients on building online businesses, I was flown to Montreal for three weeks to teach Lifestyle Entrepreneurs Academy as part of one of the most exclusive personal development programs in the world, Project Rockstar.

That segued nicely into a return trip to Malaysia and Singapore for the Asian launch of Lifestyle Entrepreneur and speaking to a couple hundred book fans as part of BookFest Malaysia in the heart of Kuala Lumpur. A group of friends from school who were studying abroad in Thailand came down for the launch and we all partied for a few days afterwards.

Then a scheduling snafu, I ended up flying from Singapore to Tokyo to LA to San Francisco to Paris to Stockholm, Sweden in 36 dreadful hours, but all was well after meeting back up with the Project Rockstar crew there and taking a party boat to Helsinki for a day before wrapping up the program in Stockholm with a grand finale dinner of reindeer and lingonberries for 25 in an underground cave like restaurant.

I made it back to San Francisco and slept for two days, then went to three weekends of back-to-back personal development and business conferences for aspiring authors. There, at an event called Author 101 University in Las Vegas, I met the Morgan James Publishing team, who are known as "The Entrepreneurial Publisher" and I knew that was the team I wanted to partner with to bring Lifestyle Entrepreneur to North America.

Just before the conference I got word that Lifestyle Entrepreneur became the #2 business best seller in Malaysia and used that as a hook to get Morgan James interested. Well, that relationship came to fruition after a few discussions (which is how this book got into your hands!) and a few weeks later it was back to Asia for the fourth time in one year to promote the book all over Malaysia.

> **This book gives you the road map, you just need to get in the drivers seat and start the engine.**

And in the middle of that trip, I met up with the instructor team from Project Rockstar in Thailand for a few days of fun off the tour circuit. So fun that we didn't want it to end. So fun that after dancing on the beach for hours and almost going to sleep we got up and headed back out to the beach to toast the coming end of an amazing year, surrounded by hundreds of others celebrating their own journeys in their own ways. All of us united by the simple fact that we're thousands of miles from home, doing what we love and doing it for a living.

That is the journey of this Lifestyle Entrepreneur, and this book is about how to set up your own life and business to have adventures like this or any other that sound most appealing to you!

Your mission is to define and design an interesting lifestyle and to step into the role of entrepreneur to bring it into being. And if that's true, then isn't it time to get more deliberate and strategic to get the most satisfaction and enjoyment from your life and work?

Well, I'll tell you what. If you don't stand up and lead the charge, no one else is going to do it for you. Yes, it's true, there are more opportunities today than ever before and the world is more interconnected and accessible than ever before, but that doesn't necessarily translate into higher wages or a more secure job working for someone else.

That means that you have to take it upon yourself to dream big and i magine a vision of greatness for your life that is really worth going for.

Then you need only the courage and fortitude to step into the unknown and claim the glory that awaits you. It is out there and it's calling your name.

Can you hear it?

Yes, setting down the road of Lifestyle Entrepreneurship can seem daunting at times. There will be times when you will be uncertain about what to do next, or even how to get started if this all sounds like a distant unattainable dream. But you need to feel the fear and do it anyway.

This book gives you the roadmap, you just need to get in the driver's seat and start the engine. Once you get going and experience the thrill of accomplishment that comes from taking action towards your dreams, all the other stuff just fades away in the rearview mirror. Just like driving at night with your headlights on, you only need to be able to see the next stretch of road, not all the way to the final destination. As you keep moving, the signs will appear and you'll get your bearings. Then you can really hit the gas and kick it into overdrive!

Sometimes it feels like my life is on fast-forward and I have to focus on staying present in the midst of bounding around the world and involving myself with the details of so many people's businesses and aspirations. So in writing this book I am thankful to have a compelling reason to reflect on all that I've accomplished in my first ten years as an entrepreneur and to package the lessons I've learned and strategies I've developed into a fun to read book that inspires and equips you to live a life of passion and purpose!

INTRODUCTION

This book is the result of having lived what many would call a non-traditional life. In my twenties, I founded or cofounded over five businesses and was fortunate enough to sell two of them.

I have been in a rock band touring America, and I've been flown around the world as a professional dating coach.

I have travelled to, and lived in, over 30 countries, learning the local languages while there. I feel very blessed to have friends all over the world, a family that loves me at home, and generally to live the life that I've always dreamed of.

But this book isn't about me. It's about You!

If you take only 10% of the information and ideas in this book and put them into practice, it will change your life. I promise.

This book contains the essence of everything I've learned over the last 10 years of starting businesses, travelling the world and exploring the things I am passionate about. Now I would like to share a blueprint for how you can do all of these things and more.

To be a Lifestyle Entrepreneur is to live life to the fullest. It means stepping up and taking responsibility for creating the life you want to live, and it means embracing a culture of life-long learning. Lifestyle Entrepreneurs want to spend as much time as possible doing the things they love by incorporating their interests and passions into businesses that amplify and support that lifestyle.

As an aspiring Lifestyle Entrepreneur you will first seek to know your own mind and heart. To truly understand your own motivations and hesitations and design your ideal identity. From there we will discuss beliefs and how they influence our thoughts, emotions and actions. These are foundational concepts that pave the way to build something truly great.

Next I will present the concept of a Vision-MAP to you. This is a model for creating new businesses and stands for Vision, Mission, Actions and Product. The Vision-MAP framework builds off of the identity and lifestyle exercises and takes them into the realm of business, giving you the tools to plan, launch and grow businesses of your own.

In the process of exploring what it means to be a Lifestyle Entrepreneur, I will share some stories from my own travels and businesses, and present the learning lessons gained these experiences. I'll also introduce you to a number of the most successful people I know who live this lifestyle, traveling the world, making memories and making an impact.

Then I will show you the tools and strategies that make it work such as using Creative Constructs to plan long term travel opportunities and how to cut down the amount of work you need to do using Threshold Theory and the Principle of The Power Hour.

It is my hope that the first half of the book inspires you to make changes to your life and work habits. In the second half of the book we'll move from the general to the specific, and explore the four types of businesses that Lifestyle Entrepreneurs use. This will allow you to focus on the type of business that suits your personality and structure it in a way where you can run it from a laptop anywhere in the world.

Then we will get into the details of launching and growing a business using The Operations Model, which is a time-tested blueprint for structuring internet-based businesses. The Operations Model looks at each moving part in your business one at a time and I'll show you how to make yours run like a well-oiled machine.

Towards the end of the book we'll look at how to manage teams around the world using online talent platforms, with the ultimate goal of setting you free to pursue your interests, confident that others are working on your behalf. For these discussions I've invited a few experts to contribute their ideas as guest authors.

Finally, we'll zoom back out and look at the big picture again. By that time your brain should be bursting with exciting new ideas.

But once the book ends, the real journey begins. There is a whole community of Lifestyle Entrepreneurs that are putting these ideas into practice every day and living their dreams.

My goal is for you to join us, and ultimately that I may learn from you and your experiences. If I've done my job right with this book, you will soon have something to teach me and I love learning!

So let's embark on your journey toward becoming a Lifestyle Entrepreneur. If at any point you are confused, or something is not clear, please write me and I'll do my best to clarify: Jesse@JesseKrieger.com

I hope that this book inspires you to live the life you have always dreamed of, and gives you the tools to do so.

Sincerely,

Jesse Krieger
Jesse@JesseKrieger.com
www.JesseKrieger.com

ps: Learn about my signature training program Business In a Weekend here: www.BusinessInAWeekend.co

pps: Join the global community of lifestyle entrepreneurs on my blog: www.LifestyleEntrepreneurBlog.com

How to

Design

The

LIFESTYLE

Of

Your

Dreams

When it comes to creating a lifestyle that fills you with a sense of purpose and excitement, there are a few guiding principles that can help start the process. The first principle is perhaps the simplest, and that is to live your life the way that feels right and true to You! It is very easy to live a life that someone else has planned out for you, or to feel like the purpose of life is to live up to someone else's expectations.

So while it may cause some friction in the short run to change gears and re-engineer your lifestyle, if your friends, family and significant others truly value your happiness, they will eventually come around and your relationships will be healthier because of it.

There were plenty of times that I chased an idea so far down the rabbit hole that I couldn't be sure I was going down the right path. But those feelings of uncertainty, coupled with a drive to succeed and prosper have always helped me persevere until I crossed enough thresholds to be taken seriously in my new endeavor.

My mother wasn't particularly supportive of me foregoing college to travel Europe playing rock music in bars and clubs. But that experience led to me owning a record label on Music Row in Music City, Nashville Tennessee. And when my band had the #1 independent rock song in USA she was our biggest fan! It wasn't that I wanted to disrespect her wishes for

> **The first principle is perhaps the simplest:**
>
> **That is to live your life the way that feels right and true to You!**

me, but rather I wanted to prove that I could make a career doing what I love, even if that meant a lot of setbacks and disappointments along the way.

During three years of playing music and running a record label with my band mate Jake, I had built relationships with people from all walks of the business world; marketers, radio promoters, video producers, investors, management firms and public relations agencies. They all dealt with me as Jesse Krieger, the guitarist for Harsh Krieger that also runs the business side of things. That was my identity for a while and I lived it 100%. But after many years we came to a point where we all wanted to experience something else in life, and we decided to disband and go our separate ways.

That was perhaps the first time in my adult life where I was conscious of the opportunity I had to create a new identity. As I was driving back to my home town of San Francisco I decided to launch a consulting firm and try to leverage all the relationships I made running a label to help other musicians and businesses. That was the beginning of Krieger Consulting Group, which still exists to this day. However the focus quickly grew from just working on music industry projects, to learning all sorts of new industries like VoIP, nutritional supplements and consumer products. I found the experience of building a company in one industry had many parallels with doing the same in any industry.

> *I saw the bigger picture: Lifestyle & Entrepreneurship as two intertwined ideas, like DNA strands circling around one another, enabling each other to grow.*

It didn't take long to feel comfortable in my new identity as a business development and strategy consultant to small, fast-growth companies. Whatever I didn't know, I would stay up late studying and gaining new skills just in the nick of time to apply them to projects. By always trying to go the extra mile for clients, I built a great referral-based business that lead to working alongside 4-time Superbowl champ Bill Romanowski. He hired me to quarterback the launch of his new nutritional supplement business. This project was the peak experience of my early years as a consultant and Bill turned out to be not only the hardest hitting player in the NFL, but also a very driven entrepreneur.

As my client's businesses began to grow and more people joined their teams, it became clear that the one thing all my clients were struggling with was raising enough funds to grow their businesses. This was a preview into my next lifestyle change as I started to build relationships with investors and investment banks that to help my clients get financing. Once I saw the world of using money to make money up close, I knew that this was where the real fortunes were lost and made, where the real action took place. Before long I was studying for my Series 7 & 63 securities licenses to become an investment banker with a boutique investment bank that offered me a VP of Business Development title in exchange for merging my consulting practice with them. I accepted.

One of my heroes has always been Steve Jobs, founder of Apple and Pixar. In a commencement speech at Stanford University he said that you can only connect the dots looking backwards. That following your passion can lead you to unexpected places, studying or working on projects that seem disconnected or random. But looking backwards, after the fact, there is a common thread that connects all of those experiences together and you'll find that you got just the right information and experiences to prepare you for the next round of challenges and opportunities.

This advice proved prescient as I embraced my new identity as an investment banker. I went into overdrive; scouting deals, on the phone at all hours, pitching investors, flying in and out of cities on the same day for meetings. I had the pedal to the floor and was making hundreds of thousands of dollars in commissions from millions of dollars of transactions I was generating.

> *But the success was not without cost, as my relationship life suffered and even my family began pointing out that when they asked "how are you?" I would start listing off the current state of prospecting, selling and closing different deals.*

Then, in the summer of 2008, I stumbled upon what looked like an once-in-a-lifetime opportunity. A community of entrepreneurs, dating coaches and health & fitness experts was putting together a pilot program called Project Rockstar.

The idea was to take six somewhat ordinary guys and break all the boundaries of what's possible in terms of lifestyle. From fashion consults and approaching attractive women in the streets to customized fitness programs and business mentoring, Project Rockstar was 56 days that challenged and replaced every conception of what I thought was possible!

> When you follow your passions, wherever unexpected places they may lead, you will inevitably stumble across some of your life purposes.

I began Project Rockstar as an introvert, determined to become wealthy at all costs and finished a new man. No more anxiety about talking to strangers or speaking in front of groups and my conception of wealth transformed as well; now I value my time and mobility above just an ever-increasing bank balance. In the process I got to travel to London, Stockholm and Shanghai with the instructor team and meet interesting, successful people from all walks of life. This was a major turning point in my life that set me down a path leading directly to this book.

Now for the last four years I have travelled the world teaching workshops on dating science, lifestyle design and entrepreneurship. The creator of Project Rockstar and now one of my closest friends, Jim Stark once said that "the best way to true understanding is to assume the role of the teacher." And so it is that I started down a road of personal development and empowerment, only to find myself now being the one doing the teaching. It is both a rewarding and extremely fun job which has led me to writing this book.

The seemingly disconnected events, the chance meetings that lead to a future business partner or relationship only really become clear upon reflection. So don't try to plan too far into the future when you're just exploring a new idea or relationship. Be open to serendipity and attuned to the possibilities that can arise out of the most unexpected of places. This is the core principle that underpins a life worth living and sets the stage perfectly for the discussion on the Lifestyle Entrepreneurs road map to follow

WHAT IS A LIFESTYLE ENTREPRENEUR?

Think of the most successful person you've ever seen. What does he look like? Who is she with? Where are they going and how are they travelling? Despite the specifics, there is a good chance they look happy and radiate a sense of confidence that is born from accomplishment. This is what a Lifestyle Entrepreneur does. They are successful people who do what they want, when they want to, with whomever they please. And they do it in style, making it look easy and inviting in the process.

Endless opportunities present themselves to the successful, as do appeals for help and aid. In both cases it is because successful people are men and women of action who are involved in a variety of lifestyle pursuits and have myriad business interests. The confidence to make the decisions necessary to be successful comes from having a positive self-image and a strong identity. It requires that you know yourself through and through, and trust yourself to make good decisions given imperfect information.

They are successful people who do what they want, when they want to, with whomever they please.

You may already have a strong set of beliefs, or a blueprint for success in one area of life. If decision making comes easy to you, then you've got a headstart on discovering, or reimagining, your identity and expressing it through your lifestyle and businesses. If not, then it really is a process of discovering your identity, by removing any covers or filters that prevent you from acting the way that feels right and experiencing happiness in your life.

Success and identity go hand in hand. You can't act in a way that runs counter to your basic values and expect to feel no guilt or shame, let alone happiness. No. Success is acting in accordance with your core values while pursuing business interests and passion projects with friends and partners around the globe. That is the path of a Lifestyle Entrepreneur on the road to mastery.

Taking inventory of your current belief system and identity is the first step towards becoming a Lifestyle Entrepreneur, so let's get started!

LIFESTYLE ENTREPRENEURS ROADMAP

Let's begin with the end goal in mind. The Lifestyle Entrepreneur's Roadmap summarizes the core concepts presented throughout *Lifestyle Entrepreneur*. Indeed, gaining an understanding of how these concepts interrelate will give you the tools to design your lifestyle and build businesses that reflect and amplify your identity, interests and passions.

These are represented by the star tetrahedron, or the Centerpiece Star. As two interlocking triangles representing the behavioral aspects of your life and what you are creating and manifesting as a result of them, this star serves as a reflection of your identity at any given time. As time goes on, interests change and life circumstances change. The Lifestyle Entrepreneur's Roadmap is a flexible tool to help you create the lifestyle and entrepreneurial endeavors you value most.

The Lifestyle Entrepreneurs Roadmap

Lifestyle	Identity	Entrepreneur
Beliefs	**Identity**	**Vision**
Thoughts	Know	Mission
Emotions	Do	Actions
Behaviors	Be	Product

THE FOUNDATION OF SUCCESS

Discovering Your Identity!

Know >> Do >> Be

*"When you **know** what you want,
it becomes clear what must be done.
As you **do**, eventually you will come to **be**.
And that is your **identity**."*

DISCOVERING
YOUR IDENTITY

Becoming a Lifestyle Entrepreneur begins with a true understanding of who you are through your identity and core values. This requires you to become self-aware and assess your current circumstances in life, and then to define and design the most compelling vision for the future you can. But before we get there, let's begin by taking inventory of where you stand today in terms of your worldview, your competencies and skills.

> Once you realize the dreams you have today, the horizon for what is possible stretches extends and new goals that may have seemed totally unobtainable will start to come clearly into focus.

To do this we will start by looking at the three internal identity drivers that inform your experience in life. These are the Mental, Emotional and Physical aspects of who you are. Collectively the internal identity drivers construct your perception of reality in terms of what you think is possible, how you feel about your life experiences and what you're physical capabilities and limitations are. These are the biological foundations of your identity.

Then we will look at how the "inside comes out" through the three external identity drivers that determine how you perceive and experience your place in the world. We'll refer to these as your psychological components, which describe what you Know, the things you Do, and the roles you play (how your show-up, or Be in the world). Collectively, the internal and external identity drivers are a function of your belief system and are the system that dictates how you see the world and how others experience you.

Following is an exercise that provides an opportunity to take an honest assessment of your biological and psychological foundations and will empower you to discover, and ultimately reimagine, your identity. It will tell you where you stand and what needs to be done to change and create the identity you really want. This is good because after getting clarity on your identity today, I want you to go through the exercise again to create your ideal identity for your future as a Lifestyle Entrepreneur. This will come about by focusing on your interests and identifying your passions, re-engineering the inward drivers of your identity so that you can support the new external manifestations, and ultimately living an entrepreneurial lifestyle of freedom and opportunity.

With clarity on the biological and psychological sides of the identity equation, all the other tools, tactics and strategies in this book will become a bridge from where you are today, to whom you'll become tomorrow. And you know what the best part is? Once you grow and realize the current dreams you have today, the horizon for what is possible stretches further into the distance and new ambitions and goals that may have seemed totally unobtainable will start to come more clearly into focus. This is the way to build momentum and go from strengh-to-strength, exceeding your expectations and serving as a role model to those around you.

You can revisit this exercise at any time, take a snapshot of where you are, and strategize for the next steps you'll take. The goal here is to be living in alignment with your interests and passions and doing it on purpose. When your internal identity drivers are aligned with your outward facing persona, actions and undertakings, well that is the sweet spot where the magic happens. This fully-expressed version of you is represented by the centerpiece star at the heart of the Identity Map. This is you living out your fullest potential with clarity and purpose, serving as an inspiration to others and making money in the process. I've seen

> **The goal here is to be living in alignment with your interests and passions and doing it on purpose.**

it happen time and time again, in my own life, in my client's lives and across the global network of Lifestyle Entrepreneurs who I deeply admire and consider some of my closest friends. The creation process never gets old.

So let's get to work! Here we will walk through the construction of each component of your Identity Map using my experiences as a case study. This should start the wheels turning in your mind so you can create an Identity Map that accurately reflects where you are today, and more importantly, where you want to go tomorrow.

THE INTERNAL IDENTITY DRIVERS
Your Biology: Mental, Emotional and Physical

Mental — The mental identity driver consists of your thought patterns and reasoning abilities. When you are thinking logically in terms of cause and effect, or thinking about the structure and blueprint that underpins a business, a language, a skyscraper or a class curriculum. All of the mental drivers reside in your mind. So when you are thinking and planning, you are engaging your mental abilities, and for our purposes here it is important to take inventory of how your thought patterns operate, and really drilling down on how you perceive the world.

For this exercise it is useful to write down 3-4 of the mental drivers you identify with wherever you are in life right now. What are the logical and rational qualities that you embrace when interacting with your friends, your family, your work colleagues or that you value in your relationships?

So grab a pencil and a sheet of paper! Finish these sentences and you will begin to get clarity on the current state of affairs for your mental identity drivers:

The intellectual challenges I enjoy most are...
My approach to planning and problem solving is...
I am most satisfied when I am thinking about...
I get my best ideas when I am...
When I think about my life a year from now the first thing I think is...
Why do I think _____ is totally unrealistic?
I think that I can....

My Mental Identity Drivers:
When I really think through the things I value most that reside in the mental sphere, I came up with these four:

Embrace a Culture of Life-Long Learning — Essentially my brain is wired to always be taking in new information and structuring it to be useful towards whatever I'm interested in and passionate about at the time (which become explicit with the external identity drivers).

Enjoy Challenge of New Languages — After spending a year living in Austria studying German and a couple years studying Mandarin Chinese in Beijing, Taiwan and UC Berkeley, it has become clear to me that I love studying languages as it gives me an expanded perspective on communications (in general) and how I interact with people in English.

Strategic Thinker — Since a young age I have always looked at situations and opportunities and projected forward how they could be elaborated and expanded. Basically, setting a strategy for accomplishing goals and minimizing things I'm disinterested in has become my default way of thinking

Crave Novelty — Scientifically, new experiences stimulate brain activity, increase neuronal connections and release dopamine, giving a feeling of satisfaction. For me, I feel the most satisfied when I'm pushing forward the frontiers of my knowledge on a number of fronts at once. I enjoy the stimulation that new sights, sounds and surroundings provide. Systematically introducing novelty gets me thinking beyond my current situation.

Summary:

The mental identity drivers (your thoughts) are the precursors to emotions and ultimately your actions, all of which are subject to your belief system. We'll cover this in greater depth in an upcoming section. For now the important thing is to take inventory of where you are at today in terms of what you find mentally stimulating and in what ways your thoughts comprise your identity.

Emotional — The emotional identity driver deals with your intuition, feelings and creative sensibilities. Emotions are essentially "energy in motion", which cause feelings and your emotional state to rise and fall. In contrast to the mental drivers, emotions are non-linear and are not subject to logic and reason. They are created by your beliefs and how your beliefs interpret events and the physical stimuli that your body receives. Emotional drivers are experienced through your intuition, your creative sensibilities and how you feel and fare in the face of challenging circumstances, as well as the feelings that accompany triumph and victory after working through them.

Much has been written about the difference between male and female brains when it comes to emotional capacity and emotional intelligence. However, it goes without saying that both men and women experience emotions, even if it shapes our identities in different ways. So no matter what gender you are, it's important to recognize that emotions are a function of your beliefs and thoughts, and influence your actions and how you're perceived by others.

Now begin to take inventory of your emotional identity drivers by completing the following sentences:

When a new opportunity presents itself I feel...

If I am excited about, but unfamiliar with, a topic/challenge I feel...

The activities that give me the greatest feeling of joy are...

Once I decide to do something I feel...

When things don't go the way I planned my emotions...

The emotional environment I grew up in could be described as...

My Emotional Identity Drivers

Here are some of the key emotions, general feelings and emotional states that influence my identity:

Feel the Fear, Do it Anyway — When I'm certain about a course of action, but ensure about how stressful and/or potentially embarrassing it will be I just go back to this mantra, take a deep breath and dive in. Every successful person has failed numerous times before ultimately succeeding, so I know I'm in good company.

Proud of Accomplishments — This is the feeling of success after putting in the work. Pride on its own may not be the healthiest emotion, but taking time to appreciate my accomplishments has never diminished them in my eyes.

Determined to Succeed — If there is one thing I am scared of it is not so much failure as it is mediocrity. Falling down in the pursuit of a passion is a learning lesson that helps know what to avoid next time; failure is not getting back up. Determination helps me get up and keep moving further towards the goal line.

Healthy Nervousness — This is a little different than the first one in the sense that being a Lifestyle Entrepreneur isn't really about surety and security; it's more about facing the unknown and wanting to know it despite a healthy nervousness or anxiety to explore new industries and interests.

Summary

Being aware of your emotional state as well as what heightens it and depresses it is a critical part of becoming a successful Lifestyle Entrepreneur. Emotions are the biological bridge between thought and action. All great performers get nervous before hitting the stage, but that feeling focuses the mind and speeds up your biology so you deliver the best performance possible. Trusting your feelings is the key to integrating mental thoughts into physical actions.

Physical — The physical identity drivers describe how you relate to the world through your five senses, how focused you are on health and fitness and your genetic disposition. Just as your thoughts impact your emotions, and your emotions affect your physical state, so can your physical health and well-being alter the way you think and feel. As we'll discuss in a later section, beliefs, thoughts, emotions and actions all impact one another and are the primary variables in formulating and maintaining your identity.

Taking inventory of your physical state includes what you do to your body and what you put in it, but also touches on what type of body you were born with. Being super tall can make people pre-disposed to say, playing basketball or needing to stretch more, while having some type of allergy or medical condition would drive a different worldview and lifestyle choices than someone without them.

Finish these sentences to start shedding some light on the physical drivers that influence your identity and lifestyle choices:

In order to stay healthy and in shape, every week I...
When choosing what to eat and drink, I focus on...
The environments and activities that make me feel energized are...
The traits I was born with that influence how I interact with the world are...
The physical traits I am most satisfied with are...
The physical traits I am not pleased with are...
To be even more healthy and fit I could focus more energy on...

My Physical Identity Drivers

Here are some of the physical drivers that influence and define how I interact with the world:

Cycling & Gym 5x/Week — Once I got serious about getting in the best shape of my life, and started feeling the benefits of doing so, this workout regimen started to fall into place. I love cycling and also getting a full-body workout in the gym. Fortunately the two are complimentary.

Mostly Healthy Diet — Yeah, that's right, mostly. I like having a few drinks and some dessert from time to time. Other than that, I'm pretty careful about not eating too many empty carbohydrates or sugar. I use vegan protein supplements and drink lots of fresh vegetable juice in the morning. By dinner time, all bets are off.

Enjoy Being Outdoors — There is something relaxing and rejuvenating about spending time outside. After a walk outdoors, a long bike ride, or a swim in the ocean it is hard not to feel good.

Dairy Allergy — Life dealt me this deck of cards, and I'm playing the hand. I used to be very allergic to dairy (like no cheese on pizza growing up and forget about ice cream), now I can enjoy these things in moderation but this allergy lead me to discover some delicious alternatives like coconut water.

Summary
The key point I want to convey here is that changing your physical state can initiate changes in your emotional state and mental state. The internal identity drivers are all interconnected in this way, and I've found that many people underestimate the impact that improving their health, diet and sleeping patterns can have on productivity and accomplishments. When I know I need to focus on something important, I'll make sure to exercise beforehand, eat healthy and get a full night sleep. Then my mental and emotional states are primed for productivity.

THE EXTERNAL IDENTITY DRIVERS
Your Psychology: Know, Do and Be
The internal identity drivers describe what's on your mind, what's in your heart and what's going on with your body. Collectively these factors influence how you feel day-to-day and start to paint a picture of your own self-image, how you perceive and experience life from the inside looking out. The external identity drivers define how you are perceived by others in terms of the knowledge you have, the activities you're involved in and the roles you play personally and professionally in the world. In the Discover Your Identity exercise they are represented by Know, Do and Be, which are the external manifestations of your internal thoughts and feelings through your physical being.

Essentially the goal of this exercise is to take a snapshot of where you are right now, today, in terms of living fully expressed and aligned with your interests and passions. Ideally, how you "show up" in the world and the things you do and pursue are an accurate reflection of your internal makeup. If something is out of alignment or some facet of your personality is not being properly expressed, well that's fine for now, and it's good to identify it, because it makes explicit the things to focus on it order to be fully aligned with your passion and purpose.

> **Take a snapshot of where you are right now, today, in terms of living fully expressed and aligned with your interests and passions.**

The first run through this exercise gives you a snapshot of where you are today and then you can create the Identity Map for your tomorrow. This gives you a clearly marked path from Point A (today) to Point B (tomorrow) and all the other tools, strategies, case studies and stories in this book help form a bridge to get you there.

Know — These are the areas where you have considerable knowledge and expertise. Whether it is because you have studied extensively to grasp the concepts, or because you have first-hand experiences that inform your understanding, these are the topics and areas of interest where you have accumulated enough knowledge to speak confidently about them.

Looking forward into the future, these are the things that you want to learn more about, understand better and eventually master. This could be skills relating to a new business venture, just as they could be areas of interest that you have simply always wanted to know more about. One of the core principles of all successful Lifestyle Entrepreneurs is to "embrace a culture of life-long learning", so dig deep and think about what topics in the world intrigue you to study, learn and attain a relative level of proficiency and expertise at.

To give you some structure and direction for identifying three to four primary areas of knowledge that you currently excel in, try finishing the following sentences:

Some of the topics that I really understand and have studied to support my career are...

The last three books I read were about these topics, or focused on this general field of interest...

One of the things I've always been passionate about and now have a solid understanding of is...

The things I actively read about, watch films or TV to learn more about or follow in the newspaper are...

The expertise that people are willing to pay me for professionally falls into these categories...

Knowledge Expressed as an Identity Trait

These are the things I'm interested in that show up externally to others in my life. The things I Know that others can observe:

Entrepreneurship — In the beginning, I turned my love of music and playing guitar into running a record label to support my band. That was learning by doing, but I have since founded a number of companies and read dozens of books on entrepreneurship (as well as written one!) so this is a fairly well-rounded area of expertise for me.

Chinese Language — From my first trip to Shanghai in 2008 to the present I have launched a wholesale USB business that manufactured in China, and studied Chinese in Beijing, Taiwan and UC Berkeley. I even won 3rd place in the California Chinese Speech Contest a few years ago, but I have since resigned this to an interest of mine, as opposed to making it my #1 career focus.

Lifestyle Design — As a function of my innate curiosity and love of new experiences, cultures and countries I have designed many interesting iterations of my lifestyle and now understand how to help others do the same. Being open to new experiences and not restricting myself with too many responsibilities in any given place or time allows me to have a fluid experience of life that blends work, play and travel.

Current Events and World History — One of the things I loved most about going to college later in life was the chance to really understand the bigger picture of what is taking place around the world now, and over the course of history. I studied Political Economy, which is essentially the study of how the world works and has worked over time as a complete system.

Summary

The extent to which you explore new areas of interest dictates how others perceive you and shapes the opinion others have of you. What you specifically choose to learn more about is a function of your internal identity drivers and is an important variable in your externally expressed identity.

Do — This is all about taking action. What do you do day-to-day, consistently over time and across the span of a year? This category describes the actions you take for your career and for personal enjoyment. These are the things you do (ideally) because they give you great pleasure and personal satisfaction, but if that's not true today then you know what to write for the next exercise. Here you want to record the actions you take that have consequence and create value in the world

What you Do is a function of your emotions (or your energy-in-motion) and is analogous to your emotional internal identity drivers being expressed outwardly. Simply put, in an ideal scenario, you would Do the things that give you good emotions and imbue you with a sense of purpose and accomplishment.

To get your mind thinking about the actions you take and the activities you're engaged in over time, try finishing these sentences:

If I were to describe the core function of my current job or business, the thing that I am hired to do is...

My daily routine consists of these specific actions...

I take the knowledge and experience that I have and put it into practice by doing these things...

One way I give back and help others is...

My favorite thing to do that is totally independent from work is...

If money, time and geography were not constraints, I would...

Actions As An Expression of Identity

Here are the top four things that I focus on doing consistently and with conviction, the areas where the rubber meets the road and I am taking action:

Launch Businesses — In the last year through Lifestyle Entrepreneurs Academy I worked alongside five clients to launch five businesses. I also launched co-founded a travel products company and a non-profit to provide funding to student entrepreneurs. It's safe to say that launching businesses is always on my agenda.

Travel Abroad Three Months Per Year — For the last half-decade it has been my focus to spend at least 25% of my life outside of my home country of America. This is at once exciting and rewarding, but it also prevents me from having a limited perspective, I always want to have a global perspective, especially since the world is more interconnected than ever before.

Create Training Products and Services — With my experience launching businesses and traveling for extended amounts of time, I turn that knowledge into training products and services (such as this book!) to help others follow the path of a Lifestyle Entrepreneur.

Fund and Coach Student Entrepreneurs — Through a non-profit I co-founded with a former classmate, University Incubator, my partner and I provide 0%-interest financing to student entrepreneurs. Our goal is to help them "create their own job by the time they graduate".

Summary

By and large you are what you do. At least in terms of your identity being externally expressed, what you do defines who you are to those around you in a big way. Conversely, if what you are doing now does not feel like an accurate representation of who you are and what you want to be, then it's time to focus on acting more in-line with how you feel inside and beginning to update some of your internal identity drivers to support a more accurate external expression through your actions day to day.

Be — These are the most easily accessible aspects of your identity. These are the roles you play personally and professionally represented by the names and titles that appear on your business cards or website. This is how you are described in any marketing language or PR that has been written about you. Essentially, these are the expectations others have of you before they meet you, based on your position, rank or title. This how you appear to others in the world.

This is the analog to your Physical internal identity driver in the sense that it is the outward appearance you give to the world. What you wear and how you act are a part of it, but it's also the qualities of character you embody and the first impression you give others before you say a word.

Finishing these sentences will give you clarity on what roles you're currently playing personally and professionally:

The word or words that best describe me are...

The primary roles I play when serving others through my profession are...

The ways I appear to others when I'm living fully expressed in my interests and passions are...

My family and friends would say that I am...

On my best days, the impression I give others is that I am...

When I am introduced to someone new, the person making the introduction would say that I am...

To Be or Not To Be...

...that really is the question! So here are the top four roles that I play in a personal and professional context. If the first time you heard of me is through this book, then these shouldn't be too surprising, but keep in mind that my Identity Map for where I'm at today is a lot different than it was five years ago and it's something I worked methodically towards since then.

Lifestyle Entrepreneur — This is my answer to the first question above, these two words describe me better than perhaps any others in the English language. This is who I am, I use the skills of entrepreneurship to design and live an awesome lifestyle, and of course it's the title of this book!

Instructor and Coach — For many years I was a professional dating coach, training guys to meet and attract the girls they found attractive. Nowadays, I'm the founding instructor for Lifestyle Entrepreneurs Academy and I coach aspiring entrepreneurs to turn their interests and passions into products and services.

Author and Speaker — These are in the same category since the majority of the speaking I do is based on *Lifestyle Entrepreneur*. When someone reads this book and comes to hear me live somewhere, it is an extension and expansion of the same content and experience.

Trusted Friend and Family Member — To my close friends, I am someone they can always count on. No matter where I am in the world, I'll jump on a call (or a plane) if one of my friends needs help. When I'm not traveling I live fairly close to my family so we can stay close despite constant changes in our lives.

Summary

How you appear to others, the impression you give off and how others ultimately perceive you is the end result of the things you know, put into practice, take action on and are consistent with over time. When you know what you want, it becomes clear what must be done. As you do, eventually you come to be. And that is your identity!

COMPLETE INTERNAL AND EXTERNAL IDENTITY MAP

Centerpiece Activities
Living Fully Expressed in My Identity

1) Write a book on lifestyle design and entrepreneurship, release it in Asia, give talks in Chinese and ultimately release it in North America

2) Focus on delivering extraordinarily valuable coaching and training both in person and through an integrated suite of products and services for aspiring lifestyle entrepreneurs

NOW IT'S YOUR TURN...

Using the above questions and examples as a guide, think through your own life and complete the exercise for yourself. Do this exercise first as a snapshot of where you are today, then again to set the stage for where you want to be tomorrow. The rest of this book will serve as a bridge to get you there!

Internal Identity Drivers

Mental:

Emotional:

Physical:

External Identity Drivers

Know:

Do:

Be:

Centerpiece Activities
Living Fully Expressed in Your Identity

 1)

2)

LIFESTYLE ENTREPRENEURS IN-FOCUS: AKIRA IGUCHI
Inspiring the Next Generation of Experts in Japan ...and Beyond

The late afternoon sun's rays reflected off the water like a million liquid mirrors, soaking the back patio of the Viking Line cruise ship with a bright orange glow. Akira stretched his arms over his head and looked back at Stockholm slowly receding into a maze of waterways as our boat pressed forward into the Scandinavian night en route to Helsinki. After five years of traveling the world learning from Tony Robbins, and ultimately becoming one of his senior trainers, Akira finally launched his own personal development book and brand in Japan and was just starting to appreciate the distance he had come.

Five years ago Akira was frustrated and lonely, studying in New York and struggling to learn enough English to complete school. Now he is in the middle of launching his latest coaching program online and as the sun dips below the horizon we all cheer as he announces that sales just passed $1,000,000! After firing off a quick congratulations email to his team back in Japan, he clicked off his phone and settled in for the overnight trip to Finland.

Akira knew from a young age that he wanted something different, something more, but he didn't yet know what that extra something was.

What a difference five years can make.

Akira grew up in a middle class family near Osaka, where his father worked as a "salary man" at a large electronics company in Japan. At a time when his culture and family encouraged him to follow the traditional path of working hard as a life-long employee at a respectable company, Akira knew from a young age that he wanted something different, something more, but he didn't yet know what that extra something was. So when he got a chance to study in New York he jumped at the chance, even though he barely spoke enough English to take a taxi from the airport to NYU.

After studying double time for months, going to classes by day and then learning what all the new vocabulary meant at night, Akira started to grasp English enough to see how ineffective many English programs are for Japanese speakers. Deciding this could be a good business idea, Akira offered a seminar called "How to Learn English Effectively for Japanese People" and got 40 sign-ups for $300 each after taking out a small ad in a Japanese-American publication. He sums up the experience succinctly, "I learned that if I act on an idea, I can really do it. And so can you."

This first brush with entrepreneurship sparked Akira's interest in personal development which lead him to a Tony Robbins seminar, and at that point he was sold. There would be no life-long employment at a buttoned-down Japanese firm, he would blaze his own trail and inspire others to be their best, training them to build businesses based on their expertise and knowledge. In short, he brought the "expert industry" to Japan.

Based on his extensive work with Tony Robbins, Akira authored the best-selling book "How to Evolve Your Life in Seven Days" and began publishing videos of him teaching personal development and marketing online. He built up a following (and email list) of over 5,000 people by just giving away free valuable content for a few months, then he offered a full training program to help people write books and build their own coaching practices. The response was encouraging as dozens of people signed up for around $2,000 each.

> Akira decided he would blaze his own trail and inspire others to be their best, training them to build businesses based on their expertise and knowledge.

Now Akira has built up a following of nearly 100,000 people in Japan and regularly offers new training programs to his community online. By partnering with a few of the top marketing experts in Japan and shooting all the videos ahead of the launch, Akira is free to travel the world, "meeting and learning from the best of the best, and going back to Japan once a month to teach a live seminar".

Akira has a personal assistant in Japan who monitors the progress on his projects and sends him a daily report of what happened, what needs to be done and what she learned that day. "The last question," says Akira, "is the most important, since it places on emphasis on growth every day and empowers her to be more than just an assistant." Structuring his business to run on short bursts of intense creativity and video production, followed by rolling out that content over a period of weeks, is what allows Akira to travel the world, running his business from a laptop.

"Last year I traveled to Singapore, Las Vegas, Tokyo, Bali, Los Angeles, San Francisco, Sydney, Monaco, London, Paris, Stockholm, Montreal and New York. The highlights were I met the coolest people on the earth in terms of their wealth, energy, inspiration, and network," he said.

As this book goes to print, Akira just sent me pictures of him partying with Richard Branson and a group of other entrepreneurs on his private Necker Island.

And how did he get there? The weekend getaway to Necker Island was part of a "Mastermind" group he joined hosted by Joe Polish, who has raised millions for Branson's Virgin Unite charity. Taking his own advice, Akira joined the group to continue his own personal development and ended up partnering with Richard Branson to grow Virgin Unite Japan!

So what is Akira's advice for aspiring Lifestyle Entrepreneurs around the world?

"Follow your passion, invest in your learning and learn from the best. Spend time with people who you want to become, be humble and be honest and do it right now!!"

TIME TO GO SUPERNOVA!
Firing on All Cylinders

Discovering your identity and identifying the centerpiece activities that give you the greatest satisfaction puts you ahead of so many others who just drift through life without taking ownership of their desires. When you consciously think through which activities and relationships should be prioritized in your life, and revisit them when circumstances change, something big begins to happen.

You will naturally become more energized as you focus more time and energy on the things that have meaning that you value. When all aspects of your life are firing in lockstep, and you build a momentum of positivity that lights up not only your life, but those around you, that is the process of "Going Supernova".

In the cosmos, a supernova occurs when a highly charged star absorbs massive amounts of energy and mass. When enough energy has been added, the star's density reaches a critical mass and an explosion occurs that is so bright it briefly outshines entire galaxies. A shockwave is created that impacts surrounding solar systems and alters their equilibrium, setting off changes in all it touches.

This is the power of concentrating your energy inward, focusing on your centerpiece and the network of allies and resources that enable it. At some point you reach a critical mass and people begin to notice a real difference in you; ***a sense of purpose that both inspires others and attracts success to yourself****.*

The centerpiece activity and the section on discovering your identity start off this book because all of the other ideas and exercises are expansions on these fundamental concepts. The centerpiece star, which represents your identity at any given time, plugs into models designed to maximize your Lifestyle and make you a formidable Entrepreneur.

LIVING BEYOND BELIEFS

THE B-TEA FRAMEWORK

Beliefs, Thoughts, Emotions, Actions

If you can dream and not make dreams your master;
If you can think and not make thoughts your aim;
If you can meet with triumph and disaster;
And treat those two impostors just the same,

If you can fill the unforgiving minute
With sixty seconds' worth of distance run,
Yours is the earth and everything that in it,
And, what is more, you'll be a man, my son.

— Rudyard Kipling

HOW DO BELIEFS INFLUENCE YOUR THOUGHTS, EMOTIONS AND ACTIONS?
=> Know the Answer and Know Success...

Every day we witness the actions of those we come in contact with. With our friends we share emotional connections. At work we deal think and exchange thoughts to solve problems. With family and in spiritual or religious contexts we relate with one another on the basis of beliefs. It may seem like these areas of life are compartmentalized and don't really overlap, such as business and religion, or how we act with family versus friends. However, I would argue that there is a common thread which ties beliefs, thoughts, emotions and actions together, and that it is a sequential process of moving from general, universal beliefs down to specific, concrete actions.

Beliefs shape your world view and are largely formed throughout childhood by the family, culture and society you grew up in. From beliefs, thoughts are formed. Thoughts are discrete packets of energy that flow from your belief system and are the precursor to all conscious action. As those thoughts move from the formless realm of the mind to impact the world we live in they are felt as emotions, or energy in motion. Emotions are physiological phenomena that cause feelings such as joy, pain, pride, and shame. They spur us to action in order to replicate good emotions or to avoid bad ones.

> Sometimes beliefs are so deeply ingrained that it is hard to imagine what it would be like to hold a fundamentally different or opposing belief.

Whether our actions are motivated by pain avoidance or pleasure realization, they are often the sole basis on which we are judged by others. So it is important to understand the motivations and culturally-reinforced beliefs that drive our actions and to change or discard any beliefs and thoughts which drive negative emotions and actions. When your beliefs enable positive thoughts, you will experience more pleasure than pain and act in a way that seeks to empower others as you enrich yourself.

HOW BELIEFS TURN INTO ACTIONS

Consider the following example. The left side shows limiting beliefs becoming negative actions, while the right side shows empowering beliefs resulting in uplifting actions.

Questions

Belief:	Belief:
I don't deserve to be successful	I deserve to be successful

Thoughts:	Thoughts:
My work isn't good enough	I do the best work I can
My boss doesn't appreciate me	My job provides learning experiences
I'm not smart enough	My opinion is valued
I'll never be as successful as them	If I work hard and smart, I'll succeed

Emotions:	Emotions:
Dissatisfaction with current situation	Content, but want more from life
Hopeless about future prospects	Optimistic about the future
Disinterest in doing more than asked	Willing to put in extra effort
Fear of rejection	Fear of a life half-lived

Actions:	Actions:
Have bad attitude at work	Positive and upbeat, fun to be around
Condescending to colleagues	Encourage and inspire colleagues
Speak softly and avoid attention	Speak confidently, open to suggestions
Do just what is required & no more	Ask for more responsibility

Do you know anyone that acts like they have limiting beliefs? Which column do you identify most with? What can you change to believe that you deserve happiness and success in life?

The Funny Thing About Beliefs is:

Whether you believe you *can* do something, or believe that you *cannot*,

Either way you are correct!

Do you know where your beliefs come from? Can you remember what it felt like the first time someone truly believed in you? Have you ever tried to change a belief that no longer served you? If so then you probably know that it is no easy task to simply change your beliefs.

Some beliefs are carried over from childhood experiences and parenting styles, while others are a result of repeated experiences that validate and reinforce a belief. In either case, if someone simply told you to believe in something different it would be difficult to reorient your mind, even if you really wanted to. That is why it is important to focus on the B-TEA framework from the bottom up; from individual, specific Actions back up to general, abstract beliefs.

My vision for this book is to empower you to live a life of passion and purpose and to build a business that supports it. Depending on your upbringing, education, experiences or any other number of factors, you may encounter internal resistance to the idea that you can literally do anything that you put your mind to. The way to gravitate towards truly believing that you can achieve your dreams is to consistently act in ways that reinforce this belief. The result of actions are emotions, and if these emotions are positive and different from what you've felt before, they will eventually affect your thoughts about what is possible and finally, through repetition, your beliefs can change.

> "Just as no one can be forced into a belief,
>
> No one can be forced to unbelieve."
>
> — Sigmund Freud

We have already gone through one exercise that can facilitate this process; the Discover Your Identity diagram. Taking an honest inventory of your interests and desires, writing them out and elaborating them into a few centerpiece activities is an example of an action that begins to chip away at limiting beliefs. This action stimulates new emotions as you imagine a life that is better in some way than the current status quo.

These emotions trigger new thoughts as your mind begins to tackle the obstacles standing between you and your dreams. Once you've worked through obstacles and hardships and experienced success and progress first-hand many times, your beliefs

> **Once you've worked through many obstacles and experienced success first-hand, your beliefs will begin to change.**

begin to change and this paves the way for further growth and progress.

This is why it is so important to simply begin taking action on your goals and dreams, even if they seem out of reach at the moment. Designing your own unique lifestyle, and becoming a true entrepreneur is not an overnight process, but one that grows with each passing week, month and year. While it certainly helps to believe in yourself from the very beginning, it is not necessary. All that is necessary is to begin taking action, and learning along the way. As time goes on and you learn lessons from all your experiences, before you know it your thoughts and beliefs will transform and support your journey even more.

CREATIVE CONSTRUCTS

Take a Break, Do What You Crave

Drop an Anchor and Ride the Waves...

Creative Constructs are temporary lifestyle changes that draw on your interests and passions to shuffle the deck in the game of life. Whether this means traveling for the summer, living abroad for half a year, participating in an intensive learning program or going off the grid and working on an organic farm for a season, creative constructs are an integral part of a dream lifestyle. Creative Constructs consist of setting parameters that let you work, learn

> **Look beyond the day-to-day responsibilities and begin to plan a future that excites you!**

and play; meet new people, relax and have an experience that is long enough to be meaningful, but not so long that you're committing to a whole different lifestyle long-term or indefinitely.

How often do you get caught up in the day-to-day activities involving your job, school, or family responsibilities? It can be difficult to see beyond the list of to-do items sitting on your desk and plan for a future that may seem out of reach or unrealistic. But don't spend all your time putting out fires and managing your current situation at the expense of planning for a future that excites and empowers you!

Take this time to imagine what your life would be like for 3-6 months, anywhere in the world, doing what you love. Think back to the Identity exercises Once you've defined a Creative Construct that suits you, costing it out and planning logistics becomes possible. Simply going through the planning process brings your dreams into focus and often times they are a lot more affordable and accessible than we initially believe.

The way to think about designing Creative Constructs is to "drop an anchor and ride the waves." In other words, plan to participate in an activity that tethers you to a specific geography, but only takes up part of your time so you're free to explore and follow new opportunities as they present themselves. Based on the Identity exercise you completed, you should aim to construct a temporary lifestyle that allows you to participate in one or more of the centerpiece activities for a duration of time.

Coming up is the story of a recent Creative Construct of mine where I participated in a 6-week business Chinese program in Taiwan as an anchor, and explored my new passion for long-distance cycling in the time off from classes. Going into the experience, I only knew for sure that I would be studying business Chinese for a few hours a day and that there would be around 20-30 others doing the same program. Left to be discovered was what exciting activities would fill up all the free time left over.

Of course it was useful to put in some time studying Chinese, which helps me be a better entrepreneur, but the real fun takes place exploring a new lifestyle and discovering what is unique about a different country. That is why it is important to design Creative Constructs that simply center you in a new place, but don't monopolize your time and energy.

All work and no play makes for a boring life!

Being a Lifestyle Entrepreneur is the solution to keep things interesting and fun.

CASE STUDY: TAIWAN
Business Chinese at National Taiwan University
Street Cycling & Business Networking in Asia

The late summer sun illuminated Guanyin Mountain on the horizon and glowed upon each ripple in the river, which snaked along the outskirts of Taipei all the way to the mouth of the South China Sea.

A tropical storm blew through yesterday afternoon leaving behind clear skies and a light mist lingering on the mangroves and foliage lining the Danshui river. After six weeks in a Business Chinese program at National Taiwan University and nearly 1,000 kilometers of cycling in and around Taipei, this was my final ride before returning home the next day. And so far the weather couldn't be better.

Starting from campus I'd drop down two blocks to the riverside park and cross to the other side of the typhoon gates which divide the bike paths and city streets. Here is a mirror image of the city, reflected in the long winding river, absent the packs of motorbikes and lines of cars on the avenue.

> After six weeks in a Business Chinese program at National Taiwan University and nearly 1,000km of cycling in and around Taipei, this was my final ride...

A patchwork of pathways that stretch from the sea to the mountains all well-paved, level and never far from the river. And by now I know them all like the back of my hand. Hands gripping handlebars and handling the wide sweeping arcs in the path with ease. Eighty five degrees and the farther I ride, the stronger the salt on this mid-Autumn's breeze.

Constructing my summer plans this year I knew that the 6-week program at National Taiwan University would be my anchor; a fixed commitment from 8 a.m.- Noon on weekdays that would count towards my Chinese degree back at UC Berkeley. Students studying abroad are generally eligible for a number of scholarships and grants, not least of which is a $550 gift from the Taiwanese government especially for foreigners learning Chinese. These covered my cost of living and are a good incentive to take on the responsibilities of this program.

And yet my days are free from noon onward, so I planned on making new business contacts on my free time and finding a fun activity to compliment my studies. That ended up being cycling.

This isn't the first time that I fell in love with long bike rides in foreign lands, back when I was 19/20, and living in Vienna, Austria I bought a used bike and

> I've been building up to today's 75km ride for the last three days, and I want to go all out so tomorrow's long flight home will pass by in a nice long sleep.

started riding throughout the city. Once I knew all the inner and out rings by heart I ventured outside the city, learning that all trains lead back to Vienna, so I could ride as far as I had energy and just hop a train back to main station, two blocks from my apartment.

Then after a month or so when my strength built up, I attempted an epic day ride from Vienna, Austria to Bratislava, Slovakia - from the capital of one country to another! I managed to make it without a map, relying on my nascent German skills to steer me right when I wasn't sure which way to go. And when I made it, finally, I sat on the edge of a castle wall and watched the sun set into the Danube river feeling like a million bucks.

It's funny how history repeats itself, as ten years later I find myself in a similar student apartment in a different foreign country studying the local language and making sense of Taiwan's topology one bike ride at a time. Back then my anchor activity was playing music and studying German, this time it's studying Chinese and building business contacts across Asia. Same principle, different practice.

Crossing over San Chong bridge, entering the long riverside park leading up to the base of Guanyin mountain, I notice there is a makeshift street market going on under the bridge. Stopping to refill on water I chat with the old Chinese lady selling drinks for 10NTD and point at the mountain telling her I want to ride to the top. She arches her eyebrows and says "better that you buy two bottles of water then" with a big smile.

Approaching the base of the mountain it's nearly noon on Sunday and the sun is blazing hot. It takes me a week or two to get used to the warm, wet summertime weather in Asia, but once I do it's hard to leave. There is something purifying about sweating out a couple gallons of water on an all-day bike ride and today doesn't disappoint.

Although I checked the maps a couple times and checked for roads up on previous rides past Guanyin, I just can't seem to find the way up today so I cross the river and head up to Danshui Lao Jie, the outdoor market on one of the northernmost peninsulas of Taiwan.

From here I can see where the island wraps around on the other side of the river and starts winding around the perimeter of Taiwan. About a half hour ride from the farthest point I can see is an archeological museum in the Ba Li district, which was the destination of our first big ride of the summer.

That trip solidified in my mind that cycling would be my wild card activity for the summer. And that decision opened up the possibility to integrate cycling into one of my other primary identity spheres; academics. While riding back from Ba Li with my classmate Mike we were talking about cycling and he casually mentioned that he took some great rides with the Cal Cycling Team.

> **While I more or less knew what to expect from the Business Chinese program before boarding a flight to Asia for 10 weeks, I didn't know what wonders would fill up the empty spaces in my schedule.**

"Wait, you're on the Cal Cycling Team?! I thought you got recruited to Cal for gymnastics?"

"Well, I was, but then after my injury biking was much easier than gym so I decided to go for it. You should join next semester, it's a blast..."

And so the seed of an idea was planted in my mind, born from a happenstance conversation in the midst of a flare up in my affair with cycling. While I more or less knew what to expect from the Business Chinese program before boarding a flight to Asia for 10 weeks, I didn't know what wonders would fill up the empty spaces in my schedule.

As it turns out I began devoting the majority of my free time to riding all over greater Taipei, urging myself on by framing it as a training regimen for joining the Cal Cycling Team when I got back to the States.

Looking out across the shining sea, thinking about my time in Taiwan and all the wonderful memories made, I added another goal to my bucket list:

Return to Taiwan and cycle around the whole island!

DESIGN YOUR OWN CREATIVE CONSTRUCT
What's Your MO (Monthly Outlay)?

The Beauty of Creative Constructs is that you choose a centerpiece activity from your identity as an *anchor*, then *explore* your surroundings and discover something new to integrate into your identity. By the end of the Construct you'll have acquired new knowledge and experience from the anchor activity and have a whole new perspective on what to do moving forward based on the discoveries made in your free time.

Centerpiece Activity

_____

Destination: _____

Anchor Activity: _____

To Explore: _____
_____
_____

	<u>Costs</u>	<u>Sources</u>
Anchor:	_____	_____
Exploration:	_____	_____

Cost of Living: _____

Duration (Weeks): _____   Monthly Outlay: _____

LIFESTYLE ENTREPRENEURS IN-FOCUS: JEFFERSON SANTOS

Founding Member and International Marketing Director for WorldVentures

The helicopter blades overhead whirred in a steady thunderous roar. Down below the magnificent Côte d'Azur unfolded beneath their feet. Miles and miles of pristine blue waters dotted with sailboats and yachts lapped gently against the shore of the French Riviera just a stone's throw from the steady procession of luxury hotels lining the waterfront. Jefferson Santos took his wife's hand and they both smiled. Smiling because this is the twentieth flight they've taken this year. Smiling because this trip is all expenses paid. Smiling because this is the life Jefferson worked towards for so long and now his season of success is in full bloom.

Growing up in Richardson, Texas it was no secret in the Santos family that money was tight. "I was raised by my single mother. She was supporting my sister and me, and sometimes she had as many as three jobs. She worked at a convenience store, she was a bank teller and she worked nights at a department store. Sometimes she would even pick up a paper route on Sundays for extra cash. Money was tight, and we knew it." But instead of bemoaning his humble upbringing, Jefferson decided at a young age that he would do something about it. Something big.

> **Miles and miles of pristine blue waters lapped gently against the shore of the French Riviera just a stone's throw from the steady procession of luxury hotels lining the waterfront.**

As soon as he was old enough to work, Jefferson jumped in with both feet and began working in a variety of sales jobs. "My first experiences in business were exciting! I had the dream ahead of me and was willing to work harder than anyone else. However, I needed to develop more skills in the "people department". My first venture was not profitable and I learned that it was NOT all about me. It's about the customer and the team. I was way too focused on myself and my paycheck," he said.

Realizing he needed some mentorship and guidance to fully realize his goals and dreams, Jefferson began to eat, sleep and breathe personal development. Reading books, attending seminars and listening to audio while driving and exercising, he assembled a team of advisors and "ultimately I learned the key lesson to success, that wealth building is a team sport. No one has ever achieved anything great by themselves. If you want to earn BIG and DO BIG you have to build a team."

> Through his journey of growth and personal development, Jefferson met others with the same drive and passion he felt.

Through his journey of growth and personal development, Jefferson met others with the same drive and passion he felt. Deciding it was time to step back in the ring and put all these new lessons into practice, he co-founded WorldVentures, a lifestyle and travel products company designed from the start to be a team building venture. "WorldVentures is to the travel industry what Costco is to retail. We have a membership model for deeply-discounted 'DreamTrips' and a network marketing structure for team building," he said.

Jefferson has a clear vision for the lifestyle he wants to live with his family, and his business is structured to support it. WorldVentures is structured so it can be run from a laptop, or even an iPad or smartphone. There are apps for training, managing your team, booking flights and hotels and even managing the cash flow from the business. So even now, with a team of over 200,000 people, Jefferson is able travel for months out of the year and can keep in touch with his team all over the world from the phone in his pocket.

"2012 was incredible!! My wife and I had a baby boy in April, but because of our lifestyle we were still able to travel to some awesome destinations. We went to Mexico, Cyprus, London, South of France, Montana, San Diego, San Francisco, Napa Valley, and more. Our son took over 25 flights this past year...crazy right?"

Here are Jefferson's top seven tips for becoming a full-fledged Lifestyle Entrepreneur:

1. Dig deep and find out why you are starting this business
2. Honor the struggle; we are all going to have a learning curve.
3. Build a dream team that can help you with your mission/project.
4. Who else is doing what you are doing or similar? Learn from them.
5. Always be curious.
6. Your goals need to involve others. Who else do your goals benefit?
7. Pay Attention, Get Excited, Never Quit!

Become

a

Lifestyle

ENTREPRENEUR

Fund

Your

Dream

Lifestyle

NAVIGATING THE 21ST CENTURY INTERNET ECONOMY

HOW TO RUN A BUSINESS FROM YOUR LAPTOP ANYWHERE IN THE WORLD

I'm unemployed.

Or at least if you're looking at unemployment statistics, I've never been counted in the employed column.

That's because I've never formally been an employee...

But that doesn't mean I haven't been working. Lost in the jumble of labor statistics and economic indicators is a relatively new class of people who earn a living through either entrepreneurship or contracting their services for compensation online.

The way I see it, the Internet enables a fundamentally different way of working and earning an income. 15 years ago the thrill of the Internet was being able to sign on with a 2400 kbps modem and find guitar tablature for my favorite songs, then queuing them up to download overnight as the connection was so slow. Now it's possible to hire, manage and coordinate teams of specialists in different countries and time zones via online platforms that enable a wide array of business functions.

With little more than well-defined job requirements, you can connect with service providers around the world to act as virtual departments within your business. This goes well beyond simply "outsourcing a call center", as that assumes there was a domestic call center beforehand...

What we are interested in here is taking advantage of the 21st century Internet economy to design new business models.

There is something innately fun in doing business this way and as a by-product you come to learn a little about different cultures and geographies as well as who

> Building businesses based on the availability of service providers around the globe, as opposed to hiring and managing only those close to you.

specializes in what, and where. I've found great graphic designers in Kosovo and Argentina, solid programmers in Ukraine and India and of course agile manufacturers and logistics coordinators in China and Hong Kong.

English tends to be the common language of international business, but learning a little about the customs and language of the people I've worked with has built some goodwill and facilitated working relationships with a personal touch, as opposed to focusing exclusively on the task at hand.

In most cases where continuity of the working relationship is crucial, I'll insist on working with a team as opposed to an individual. This way I can build a relationship with the project manager and then communicate with team members doing the day-to-day work on my project.

Once the framework of the working relationship is in place in the form of a Service Level Agreement (SLA), then it is not important who is executing on the deliverables so long as they get done on time, on budget, and at the level of quality I expect. This allows for broad operating latitude on both our ends and eliminates any urge to micromanage or spend more time than is necessary to get a project done.

Here is an example of how to design a new logo like this:

Using a site such as Elance.com, you can easily post a job seeking logo designers. Normally I'll make a rough sketch of my ideas, reference a few other logos on the web and describe which aspects are appealing. Then I'll ask the design team to create 4-5 variations of the hand drawn sketch that I scan and upload to the project's online workroom.

Usually I'll ask the designer to create 2-3 designs based on my sketch and give them creative freedom to design a few more based on their own creative intuition. This keeps the possibility open that you'll be pleasantly surprised by a design idea they come up with that wouldn't have otherwise been seen.

> Ask for specific deliverables, but always ask for 1-2 creative ideas of their own. This encourages creativity and you may be pleasantly surprised

Once the initial sketches designs are completed I'll look for various elements in the logo that I like and write feedback asking them to incorporate various aspects from the initial designs into a new round of logos based on my feedback. This is an iterative process where each round of designs helps clarify the idea I have in mind and informs the directions I give the designer for the next round of improvements.

Generally going through this process 2-3 times gets me 80-90% of the way there and then the final changes usually revolve around changing font styles, adjusting color schemes and the placement of elements within the logo. Having a basic working knowledge of Photoshop allows me to try ideas out and play with the placement of elements, although describing the changes that need to be made accomplishes the same goal.

> Being a Lifestyle Entrepreneur is about distilling projects down to specific tasks and drawing a clear distinction between where the entrepreneur's responsibility ends:
>
> Reviewing designs and providing feedback
>
> ...and where the service provider's begins:
>
> Incorporating feedback and creating new designs.

I find that if I look at the new ideas the designer submits for five or ten minutes and then do something else for a couple hours, when I log back in to give the designer input for the next round of redesigns I have clarity on what I'm looking for. Factor in that each round of redesigns takes a day or two to complete and this example is illustrative of the kind of Lifestyle Entrepreneurship I enjoy.

*Designing a logo, which is the basic identity for a business, should take around two weeks front-to-back, **but the actual time spent working on it is a few hours at most**, chunked into 15-30 minutes sessions of design review and writing feedback and further instructions.*

I enjoy being able to focus intently on the task at hand for a brief amount of time, then turning my attention elsewhere confident that a professional designer is incorporating my feedback and working up a new round of designs per my specifications.

In terms of lifestyle, notably absent from this process are meetings, conference calls and any kind of office politics. I know companies that spend thousands of dollars and countless hours in meetings deliberating on a "new corporate identity" with a team of designers that come into their office to present each round of redesigns in person. This is horribly inefficient not to mention a huge waste of everyone's time. When you factor in commuting times, latecomers to meetings, competing personalities and perfunctory small talk in meetings, the time expended far exceeds the benefits gained.

By carrying projects out online you regain so much of your time, and the nature of reviewing work, pondering next steps and providing creative input is in itself a fun proposition. It's akin to focusing on the essence of what creates or adds value in a business and delegating everything outside your core competencies to a team of professionals who focus exclusively on those areas. In a word, it's empowering!

Perhaps the best part is this:

Once you get used to working in small bursts of focused effort it is easy to manage multiple projects simultaneously. So now let's say I'm building a whole website using a few different service providers at once. Now my logo is done and I have a firm idea of the graphical look and feel for my new website. I can hire a graphic designer, a copywriter for the site content and a web developer for the programming work at once, each in a separate Job on Elance.

Once I provide the initial direction and instructions to each and work is underway, I can spend an hour in the morning reviewing what each provider submits then go out and enjoy the day. Subconsciously my mind is processing what ought to be done to improve the work submitted and later in the afternoon, once I have a good idea for what the next steps should be, I sit down at the computer again and spend 30-45 minutes writing out action items for each provider.

Then the ball is in their court and I've contributed my share of the responsibility until they return with questions or submit the next round of work for review. This back and forth creates time bridges where no action is required (i.e. free time) but the fact that a project is ongoing creates an interesting effect that is an exciting aspect of Lifestyle Entrepreneurship.

Perhaps you've noticed that when you learn a new word, all of a sudden you start noticing it everywhere? The same is true for learning about a new culture, place, actor or musician. All of a sudden you've discovered a new idea and it's like invisible antennas go up picking up on information that was always there but you never noticed.

The same thing happens with projects carried out online that have free time in between when you need to make contributions. Whether you're designing a logo, creating sales copy for a website, developing a product idea or incorporating new elements to a website you begin to see the world through new eyes. Things pop out as pertinent to your business and even mundane details like how products are arranged at a coffee shop can trigger new ideas like resolving an unanswered question about your website layout.

If you're starting a business while still working for someone else, this feeling will be a happy replacement for worrying about office politics and your boss's expectations. If you're starting your first business young, then the prospect of going to work for someone else starts to feel like taking a big step backwards the more progress you make on your own venture.

Ultimately, Lifestyle Entrepreneurship is about integrating your interests and exploring your passions in the context of making money, and nothing is more rewarding than becoming financially independent by virtue of your own efforts while adding value to other's lives in the process.

This is the empowering aspect of being a Lifestyle Entrepreneur:

By being in control of your life & making money you begin to recontextualize experiences, relationships and the details of daily life through the filter of "how can this help my business?"

THE VISION-MAP FRAMEWORK
Vision, Mission, Actions, Product

Learn to Become a Successful

Lifestyle Entrepreneur

...Even in Tough Times

It All Starts With a...

VISION

"If one advances confidently in the direction of his dreams, and endeavors to live the life which he has imagined, he will meet with success unexpected in common hours."

— Henry David Thoreau

"The Best Way to Predict
The Future Is To Invent It."

— Alan Kay, Computer Scientist at Apple

Setting Your Vision:

In order to take advantage of the V-MAP Framework, you must start by defining a vision of where you want to be. Your vision is something to be pursued, an illustration of what ultimate success in your business means to you. For our purposes the goal is to use the results of the Identity exercise as a starting point for deciding what type of business to create. Depending on your objectives and personality the vision for your Lifestyle Entrepreneurship business could be one of the following:

- To own a profitable business that provides enough disposable income to travel in style for three months every year, and allows the time to do so.
- To operate a market-leading business in an industry that is personally interesting, and to work with engaging, interesting people every day.
- To participate in the economic trade-flows between China and USA, profiting while attaining a better understanding of Chinese languages and culture.

Your vision statement describes the pot of gold at the end of the rainbow; it is the idea of greatness you possess; it is your creativity! The mission, actions and product elements describe the manner in which you will pursue your vision, what routes you'll take, and what to do if you get lost, respectively.

One of the most important considerations in creating a vision statement is your belief system. Creativity has no bounds and if your culture or upbringing has limited your outlook on what is possible in life, then your vision statement will fall short of its true worth. So, even if it is "just for fun" at first, try to envision an endgame that would make you totally satisfied, regardless of whether you think it is logically possible at this point.

To paraphrase one of my most gracious business mentors Michael Doyle, author of best-selling book *How To Make Meetings Work*, the future is uncertain and ambiguous. Since we don't have a good way of predicting the future, we might as well invent what we want to exist, as well as define how we will get there. We may have to go through some tough learning experiences and overcome some obstacles, but that's par for the course when you want to create something where before there was nothing:

> *"Visions are different from plans, as a vision is larger than any of an organization's plans. It ennobles. It's worth going for. Plans and strategies are often intellectual exercises and don't excite and ennoble the way a vision can. A vision gives you a sense of higher purpose to fall back on should you become mired in the day-to-day operations. You know you have a clear vision when people say "That's exciting!" When you would be willing to give your best efforts for a certain amount of time to achieve it."[1]*

Another way to approach creating a vision is to do it on a rolling basis using your Creative Constructs as near term visions to be realized. How would you spend your days? Where would you be and with whom? Doing what? If you can start to answer these questions in a way that makes you genuinely excited then you have begun to define a vision. Now you can refine your research and continue filling in the blanks on your Monthly Outlay (MO) worksheet. These figures become your targets that you organize your Actions and Product functions around actualizing.

Nothing Can Stop You When You're On a...

MISSION

---

1   Doyle, Michael. Organizational Visioning: An Old Art or a New Science? ©1989

> *"There is one quality that one must possess to win, and that is definiteness of purpose, the knowledge of what one wants, and a burning desire to possess it."*
>
> — Napoleon Hill

Build The Blueprint for Your Success:
The Mission Statement

A mission statement is the energy you put behind your vision. A mission statement engenders a business with a sense of purpose, and a reason for existing. It states your value system and what you stand for; the energy behind your vision. Your mission touches on the people, resources, functions, and processes that you set up in order to actualize your vision.

In building your Lifestyle Entrepreneurship business you will interact with customers, suppliers, contractors, and perhaps investors and employees, all of whom have their own set of expectations and objectives in dealing with you. Your mission is a set of guiding principles that lets others know what they can expect in their interactions with you.

A good mission statement shares your values and what you stand for as a business.

To be effective the mission should unite the actions of every moving part in your business, tying them together with common purpose, and focusing them towards a specific goal. When you proactively define the ways in which you will add value to others, and the terms on which you are willing to deal with them and then you are already half way to your goal!

Once you have a vision of where you want to be, and a mission that defines how you will get there, then you are 50% through the V-MAP Framework and all that is left is to execute on your plans through your Actions to create the end Product.

To really be effective, a good mission statement takes into account the naturally occurring processes of creating and manifesting. Many authors have written books on the concept that when you go with the flow, things are effortless and that things seem magical in their unfolding.

Going with the flow is another word for being in alignment with the embedded energy patterns in the Universe. It is about recognizing the principles of fractality, alignment, coherence and resonance. These terms have their roots in science, but they apply to business because knowledge of conserving and applying energy is the essence of success. These are important concepts, so let's look at them in a little more detail.

- **Fractality** - The concept that all things in life are self-similar, just on a different size and scale. In business, this is equivalent to saying that the process for fulfilling an order for a small customer should be the same for fulfilling an order for a massive customer. The procedure is the same, but the magnitude varies. Your mission states the principles that you will employ and act on in situations both large and small.
- **Alignment** - This means that your actions are aligned with your stated goals and objectives. You say what you mean, and you mean what you say. Acting in alignment, over time, is what builds a solid reputation. When you have acted in alignment, customers or stakeholders are more likely to give you a break when something inevitably goes wrong. Conversely, acting out of alignment with your mission breeds distrust and can have pretty negative consequences.
- **Coherence** - Being consistent, clear and concise is what coherence is all about. Customers, employees and stakeholders should be able to understand what you mean, without inference or guesswork. This is about being a good communicator.
- **Resonance** - When something "just clicks" and you feel an immediate attraction or kinship to an idea or person, this is resonance in action. Resonance, in physics, is the concept that two like waveforms amplify (while two opposite waveforms cancel each other out). In business, when customers and stakeholders resonate with your value proposition, they get excited and engage with your business to a greater degree, perhaps telling friends or providing testimonials.

No business is successful if the energy that is produced is self-destructive. Energy that is put into the products and services that you bring to market must be in alignment with the behavior of the employees' actions and the way things work on a social and spiritual level. In other words, if you are not truly adding value with your product or service and making clients comfortable doing business with you, eventually your business will unravel and fail.

This is because every business is a social activity that requires having people either work for you as well as interact with your product or services. Having integrity

> Business is a social activity that requires having people work for you as well as interact with your product or services.

and a strong moral fiber enables others to relate to what you produce. What goes around comes around. It has been proven time and time again that if you treat people the way you want to be treated, then there is a higher chance they will extend you the same courtesy. It is even the golden rule in the Bible.

The mission statement is one's recognition of what is important and what you are dedicating your time and resources to. Being clear is one of the key points in making things happen especially in having people work for you. If you want someone to be an integral part of your business, you must tell them what is expected of them and then incentivize them through compensation and other benefits that ensure the results you want. All of this is a component of the company's mission statement.

In the end, your business will be recognized for is the quality and usefulness of your products or services, how you treat your employees, and the satisfaction of your customers.

Seeing your dreams come true is the end result of V-MAP and is the Product component of the equation. However to get there, you must carry out the Actions that comprise your business as this is the execution of your vision and mission statements and the core of becoming a Lifestyle Entrepreneur.

Once the Planning is Done, You Must Spring Into...

ACTION

*"I have been impressed with the urgency of doing.
Knowing is not enough; we must apply. Being willing is
not enough; we must do."*

— Leonardo da Vinci

"The Ancestor of Every Action is a Thought."

— Ralph Waldo Emerson

Take Action On Your Mission to Realize Your Vision

This is where the rubber meets the road. Vision and Mission describe your business in conceptual, abstract terms, the Actions and Product components of the V-MAP Framework are tactical and action-oriented. The second half of this book is primarily Actions and Product focused.

Whether your vision is owning a business that runs on auto-pilot, or working hard and running a high-growth international company, the practical activities necessary to actualize that vision are laid out in this book.

Actions describe the operations necessary to launch and grow your business. Once we have defined the product or service you'll be offering, we'll plug those offerings into a useful business architecture called The Action Plan. This is a blueprint for internet-based businesses I have developed over the years and we'll look at it in depth in the next section.

Your task is to identify, record and systematize the functions that support your specific business with the ultimate goal of compiling a training manual describing the processes involved in running your business. With an online business and a training manual that shows others exactly how to run it, you can begin to remove yourself from daily operations and focus more on lifestyle.

Before we dive into the details of building a business, a brief look at the nature of Actions within the Vision-MAP framework will be helpful. Actions are essentially the nuts and bolts of what your vision and mission statement sets forth. To properly understand actions in this context, you need to look at your business as a set of processes and functions that must work seamlessly together to be efficient and reward the people and stakeholders involved.

You should approach building an online business with a systems-thinking mind-set. That means looking at each action and considering how it fits within the broader context, and how it can be executed more efficiently. A good goal is to systematize the actions that make your business run and then delegate them to others, so you can focus on living Creative Constructs and following your interests and passions. Systematizing the operations of a business allows management by metrics; simply measuring the performance of others against your expectations and making adjustments until it runs just right.

Consider the analogy of a healthy body, a system consisting of sub-systems like organs, arteries and a central nervous system. Your Vision and Mission make up the DNA of your business, while the organs and arteries are the departments and cash flows are the lifeblood that bring it all to life. Just as a healthy body has faster response and recovery times, the extent to which all actions are coordinated and the speed that they are executed determine the efficiency of your business system.

> Discover which actions prove to be efficient and profitable. Then you can systematize the processes into discrete functions that can be carried out by others.

View your business as a system comprised of sub-systems within which employees execute Actions. The nature of the 21st century Internet economy, as we'll see in more detail soon, is that there are hundreds of thousands of teams and contractors at your disposal around the globe who stand ready to carry out well-defined processes for very competitive fees.

I've always been a visual learner and remain a firm believer that diagrams, models and blueprints convey concepts and ideas much better than just words on a page. Visualizing how systems work or how interests overlap to reveal centerpiece activities gives you an understanding of big picture prior to diving into the details of how each component works and connects to the others. The next section will present a new exercise that will help you decide what type of business to launch. Then we can plug that into the Action Plan and launch the business that will finance your lifestyle.

When All is Said and Done You'll Have the Finished...

PRODUCT

*"The achievements of an organization are the
results of the combined effort of each individual."*

— Vince Lombard

"Results? Why, man I have gotten a lot of results, I know several thousand things that won't work. "

— Thomas Edison

The Product of your Actions should reflect your Mission, in pursuit of actualizing your Vision. You can only examine the product of your actions after the fact; everything else is planning and preparation. The product, or actual outcome of carrying out actions, affords you an analytical measure that pairs actual results against expected results in hopes of identifying areas for improvement and optimizing performance for maximum profitability. When your business is operating in compliance with the precepts laid out in your mission statement, then you have a successful business, and will no doubt realize your vision in due time.

Here are some examples of analyzing the Product against your Vision:

- Setting a target conversion rate for turning website visitors into sales leads, then monitoring the actual conversion rate and making adjustments to site content in order to improve conversions.
- Keeping accurate financial records in order to track revenue growth and profitability month-over-month.
- Benchmarking your team's response times to customer service requests against competitors' times to discover whether improvements need to be made.
- Featuring a new product on your homepage, then tracking the sales compared to previously featured products in order to gauge product popularity with customers.
- Setting sales quotas before each month and measuring the performance of each member of the sales team afterwards.

THE VISION-MAP FRAMEWORK

What the Mind of Man can Conceive
and Believe, It Can Achieve"

— Napoleon Hill

Now that we have looked at each step in the Vision-MAP framework, think back to The Lifestyle Entrepreneur's Roadmap and notice how the hierarchy of ideas translates through each concept. At the high-level our beliefs influence our identity and how grandiose a vision we're capable of conceiving. Once there is a worthy Vision in place, the MAP can be thought of as the roadmap to becoming a Lifestyle Entrepreneur. While the ability to think big and hold a vision of greatness for the future is a function of our belief system, the Vision-MAP framework is the Roadmap to actualizing that vision in the world.

From my experience there is a back-and-forth flow between our belief system, to our lifestyle and conception of identity at any given time and through to what we create and do in the world. Then as new experiences unfold, new knowledge is gained and relationships are formed, our identity shifts and our beliefs are impacted with new reference experiences that either reinforce, or run counter to, our existing beliefs. Being aware of these energy dynamics, and truly, in control of them to the extent possible, is what being a Lifestyle Entrepreneur is all about.

The Interplay Between
Belief Systems, Identity and Creating Businesses

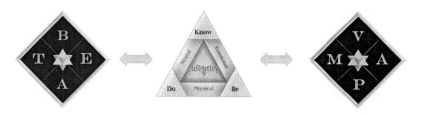

LIFESTYLE ENTREPRENEURS IN-FOCUS: JIM STARK
Affiliate Marketer and True Global Citizen

Jim is an Asian entrepreneur who grew up in Australia and eventually moved to the UK. He was brought up by his parents to work in a career in investment banking and/or law. These were, after all, what almost everyone wanted to do – the "glorious" jobs. After a brief internship at Macquarie Bank and a stint at Rothschild, Jim looked up at those older and "more successful" bankers and realized that he didn't want their lives. They seemed to be working harder and longer, making more money (which wasn't even "big" money) with no time to enjoy it. And they seemed deeply unhappy. It seemed as if everyone had bought into "a bullshit story of the best way to live your life", as Jim says. Jim wanted to be in control of his own career and lifestyle, not simply be higher up on the corporate ladder.

> Jim wanted to be in control of his own career and lifestyle, not simply be higher up on the corporate ladder.

In school he tried his hand at entrepreneurship, coordinating alumni events for different schools in Australia. Although the business got some traction, Jim "quickly learned the value of market research, as it turns out most schools coordinate alumni events internally." This business unsurprisingly failed. Through University Jim tried his hand at other businesses, which also ultimately failed.

He felt that Australia did not have the entrepreneurial culture that would help him succeed. After a brief stint travelling to Africa and learning to be a monk, seeing the Taj Mahal in India and travelling through Asia, Jim moved to downtown London and built a number of businesses, as well as a global network of friends and entrepreneurs. One of his first ventures was launching a nightclub promotions business with a group of friends, which opened up doors to exclusive clubs, beautiful girls and well-heeled businessmen. "Although I had mentors, in the end I still had to do and experience it all myself." And that suited him fine as each new venture's rise and fall filled in one more piece of the puzzle until he discovered the world of affiliate marketing and leveraged all his skills and experience to build an online empire he manages from his laptop.

Tapping his network, Jim befriended some of the most successful affiliate marketers and learned the business top-to-bottom. Traveling to conferences, coordinating meet-ups and always willing to share what he learned with those around him, Jim built a close-knit team of four. "We get together for 3-4 months a year and the rest of the time we travel. I taught them everything I know about the business and they are on a sliding scale of payment such that, at the last scale, they are basically partners. We share everything and act like a company as well as a group of people who are passionate about what we do. We are all very close."

When the business began to take off, Jim recalled some sage advice he received years before;

"Focus when you're hitting. The first time I ever made $3,000 in one day; I didn't know what to do and just stopped working. I lost that money. Nowadays I'm nearing 20x that amount in daily net profit and I'm a lot more focused."

When he finds a good offer and promotions are going good, Jim doubles down and focuses even harder on how to amplify that success. And it's working. As this book goes to print, Jim and I just toasted to him making his second million dollars... at the age of 30!

Although in the last year he has traveled from LA to the UK, from Cyprus to Australia and from Poland to Las Vegas, Jim warns "this can be deceiving - travel and business are not usually compatible. You achieve things by focused work, taking action and surrounding yourself with great people from your industry."

So what is Jim's advice to aspiring Lifestyle Entrepreneurs? "Don't travel too much initially. Instead, work hard, do your time, focus and make your money. The whole 'working and traveling' thing is bullshit if you're not already well established. It takes work and focus to become well established and this is hard to do while traveling all the time. Once you're well-situated however, you can structure your business for remote success."

As Jim and I order another round in San Francisco his eyes light up as he tells me about the lineup at Coachella this year and the party he was at in Miami last week, and the trip he's taking to Australia in a few weeks. No doubt he has arrived at the place most aspiring entrepreneurs long to be; debt-free and financially secure with a global network of friends and the world a vast landscape of opportunity.

> No doubt he has arrived at the place most aspiring entrepreneurs long to be; debt-free and financially secure with a global network of friends and the world a vast landscape of opportunity.

Of all the featured Lifestyle Entrepreneurs in this book, I owe a special debt of gratitude to Jim Stark. Not only have we traveled the world together, worked together on a variety of businesses and coached others to lead lives of passion and purpose, but Jim continues to serve as a living inspiration to me for what is possible in life. Truly a citizen of the world and one of the most successful people I know in my peer group, I can't wait to see what he'll do next, knowing full well that it will be even bigger and better than all he has done before. So, thanks Jim and keep living the dream!

THRESHOLD THEORY

Accomplish More

and Increase

the Value

of Your Time

THRESHOLD THEORY

Ideation - Development to Launch - Launch and Growth
Thresh·old noun [thresh- hōld, thre- shōld]

    a : *The minimum intensity or value of a signal, etc., that will produce a response or specified effect.*

    b : *A level, point, or value above which something is true or will take place and below which it is not or will not.*

A threshold, simply put, is the point after which it is easier to continue going in the same direction then to expend energy changing course. We want to cross thresholds in each entrepreneurial action that we undertake so as to build momentum and lock in gains from time spent working. This enables us to work more efficiently and frees up time for pursuing lifestyle goals. Crossing thresholds is the driver of progress in entrepreneurship, raising the bar with each pass and setting an additional incentive to keep motivation high and excitement present. The process is analogous to going more than half way in nearly any activity; it would take just as much energy to go back as to continue moving forward.

Threshold Theory describes the modus operandi for entrepreneurship in its primary phases:

    Ideation - The initial conceptual phase of entrepreneurship

    Development - Ideas take form and become products and services

    Launch - The infrastructure is in place to make the initial sale, and

    Growth - Sales are taking place, employees and stakeholders are engaging your ideas and the business model is refined and evolves.

Taking The First Steps Towards Starting a Business
THE THRESHOLDS OF IDEATION

Often times the most challenging thing for first-time entrepreneurs is getting started. Sometimes it can seem like starting a business is like staring at a blank page and wondering what the first words should be. Fortunately, getting over this threshold is easier than it looks. The trick is to take your initial idea (any idea) to a point where someone else could feedback on it. This is the process of manifestation; taking an idea without form, residing in your mind as an exciting thought or a blurry image of what could be, and bringing it down to earth and giving it form.

> **Crossing the first threshold is simple:**
>
> **Take your initial idea to the point where someone else can provide constructive feedback.**

The form can be a sketch on paper if it's a product, a logo with a tagline that describes the business, a one-page description using the V-MAP process or simply identifying the people and skills needed to bring your idea to life. The important thing is to do.

At the early stages you can iterate numerous times before you need to lock in a final decision to progress forward. Let your mind run free, in all directions, but before you run out of steam get something down in physical form that serves as a record of your efforts. Pulling your idea out of thin air and giving it some tangible form is the first threshold you cross on the path to entrepreneurship.

Even though you may not want to share it with anyone else just yet, it is essential that you give your idea form so you can look at it the next day with some perspective. When you have spent time and energy on an idea that is exciting and portends a lifestyle change, your subconscious is at work even as you engage in other activities.

The next day, when you revisit what you created, often times the next steps become immediately apparent. It is almost an automatic response. And if it's not in the beginning, I assure you it becomes one in time. Putting in some effort every day builds momentum and entrains your brain to build new neural networks that support the creative process of ideation.

With time these neural networks strengthen and expand, connecting to other knowledge and stored experiences in your mind thereby broadening the scope and

> **Starting a new business simply requires putting in the work, consistently, for a period of time. No prior experience is necessary.**

depth of thoughts which you can draw upon and relate back to your entrepreneurial activities. The continuity of spending some time on entrepreneurship every day (as opposed to a marathon session followed by a week of downtime) is what builds momentum and genuinely puts you into the mind-set of an entrepreneur.

Bridging that gap is no more difficult than making it a priority for an hour or so a day at the outset and ensuring that by the end of each power hour you have some tangible result of your efforts. In the initial Ideation phase some examples of crossing thresholds are:

- Sketching a product design or researching products comparable to what you have in mind and creating a new file to store images.
- Drawing a logo and writing a tagline that describes your business idea.
- Identifying websites offering similar products or services and contacting a sales representative posing as an interested customer with some questions before buying.
- Contact the marketing department for a magazine or website that caters to the industry you're considering entering. Tell them you're considering advertising and request a rate card. This is an easy way to get demographic information on the audience they reach.

Giving Your Idea Form and Making it Real
THE THRESHOLDS OF DEVELOPMENT TO LAUNCH

After working through the Ideation phase and coming up with a working concept for your business, the thresholds take on a new form. In the Ideation phase you can largely operate on your own authority, working on developing your product offering, and reviewing your work later to continue making improvements.

Once you have the idea in place it's time to start contracting service providers to build the business architecture that will manifest your vision. In this phase the threshold you should aim to clear each time you work is to provide feedback and input to your team members sufficient for them to work on

> The second step is to enlist others to develop your idea into a workable form.
>
> This means sourcing service providers from online talent platforms like Elance.com

action items you outline. The threshold is handing off responsibility to someone else with a clear understanding of what you want them to accomplish.

The Development to Launch phase is exciting as you begin to see your idea take shape and involving other people like developers, graphic designers and copywriters somehow makes the experience more "real" than when your idea is just in your own mind.

The initial steps in this phase involve defining projects that service providers can bid on, qualifying providers and negotiating terms of your engagement leading up to hiring a provider or a team. Online talent markets such as Elance.com provide an intuitive platform to carry out all these steps.

There is some overlap between the Ideation phase moving into Development. For example, if you sketch out a website design on a piece of paper and scan it into your computer that could be one work session. You can then post a project online soliciting bids from graphic designers to illustrate your sketch and provide 3-4 graphical mock-ups of what your website homepage could look like. A day or two later, after providers have bid, you can go through and respond to the ones who look promising, moving the discussion forward towards selecting a provider and the terms under which they will work. Finally, you award the project, fund an initial milestone into escrow and wait for the first round of designs to hit your inbox.

> **Become comfortable using online talent markets.**
>
> **It lowers the bar for leveraging talent in the Ideation phase, and lowers your costs in the Development to Launch phase.**

The three phases I've outlined for thresholds are meant to be guidelines, not hard-and-fast rules of the road. Becoming comfortable using online talent markets and identifying teams that do good work for you lowers the bar for incorporating service providers in the Ideation phase, and lowers your costs in the Development to Launch phase.

In terms of Ideation, this can take a form of having a design team at the ready so you can bounce ideas off them for a pre-agreed upon price per design. This cuts the time of posting a new job and qualifying a new round of providers for each project and gives you a degree of certainty as to the quality of work you'll receive.

For Development phase work, you can begin to bundle deliverables with one team once you build some working relationships online and have a working history that makes providers comfortable competing for your business. An example of this is hiring a copywriter who also has basic web development skills to write site content as well as publish it in a basic website that they create as part of the project.

Then when you hire a web developer to build out the entire site you are already past the starting line and costs go down accordingly. We'll go into these tricks of the trade later on, but you should notice the trend that working with thresholds, building relationships with online provides and eventually entering service-level agreements accelerates your entrepreneurship and decreases costs.

Going Live and Scaling Up
THRESHOLDS IN LAUNCH AND GROWTH

The idea of thresholds takes a new form when applied to the Launch and Growth phase as two new types of stakeholders begin to enter the picture; customers and contractors (or employees).

Ideation and Development activities are a one-person show from the Lifestyle Entrepreneur's perspective in the sense that anyone you engage with in those stages is likely an external contractor (i.e. online service providers). Launch, by definition means that customers come into the picture, and at some point you'll likely bring team members into the fold that are working inside your business. Your responsibilities as an entrepreneur change when interfacing with these stakeholders, and the tools of Threshold Theory adjust to meet the challenge.

The value proposition you make to customers largely determines the questions they will ask in the sales process. Even if your product offer can be completely transacted online, potential customers will still ask questions. The best way to employ Threshold Theory in this regard is to batch customer responses into a certain block of time in your day so when you are responding to all queries that came in that day you can pick up on common themes.

> As you notice themes emerge, take a moment to think of the proper course of action and institutionalize the response so repetitive work is avoided down the road.

Inevitably customers will ask similar questions, so when you notice recurring questions it means that you need to revise the marketing language visible on your website, add a comprehensive answer to a frequently asked questions document (FAQ), or update the Terms of Service section of your website.

Threshold Theory comes into play in this situation by taking action to address the root of the recurring customer questions instead of simply answering a bunch of similar emails. The early stages of launching your business is the right time to quickly iterate and fix any ambiguities in your website content and product offering.

As you go through custom emails and identify a common theme, take the time to definitively address the issue and then institutionalize it by either adding it to an FAQ or modifying the website content that causes confusion. This way you'll head off future work by solving the issue and/or have a stock answer to refer customers to. The same holds true for post-sale questions from customers.

Create a Sales and Customer Service Manual

Aside from creating and updating an FAQ and Terms of Service section of your website, the way to institutionalize responses for employee training purposes is to create and maintain two living documents; a Sales Manual and a Customer Service Manual.

Once a similar situation or issue occurs a few times you can safely assume that it will continue to do so. The identification of a recurring theme indicates that you should cross the threshold of institutionalizing a process to address it in your Sales or Customer Service manual. Over time these documents will contain a wealth of information specific to the operations of your business and be an invaluable resource for training new employees and contractors.

These documents are "living" in the sense that you date them and send out updated versions to everyone using them once material information has been added or changed. You will be increasingly free to pursue your ideal lifestyle if you maintain up-to-date manuals that are the first go-to resource for internal workers that have questions. Always leave the option open for them to contact you for any uncertainty, and then based on those questions, refine the manual further so it can solve the problem next time.

Here are some examples of recurring themes that can be institutionalized into your manuals for customer service and sales:

1. Customers routinely ask for volume discounts on products: Take the time to create a volumetric discount schedule that is in line with volume discounts you receive from suppliers. Respond to customers with the quantity they asked about, and the next two breakpoints above it. For example, if a

customer requests 25 units and asks about volume discounts, respond with the price-per-unit for 25 units and quote them for 50 and 100 units if those are the next quantity breakpoints.

2. Customers routinely ask about warranty and return policy: Understand what warranty and return policy is offered by your suppliers and mirror that as a starting point. This way you don't take on additional liability and can facilitate replacements via your suppliers. Clarify language in your Terms of Service and perhaps make the policy more visible in the marketing language on your website (ex: 1-year Warranty & 60-day money back guarantee).

3. Sales representatives ask for higher commissions or higher pay: Take time to create a graduated commission schedule based on sales milestones that encourage them to sell more in order to receive a higher or percentage of overall sales for the month. If you have multiple sales representatives, create a monthly bonus for the top performer and an additional bonus if the same representative wins three months in a row.

4. Customer Support representatives complain that customers are dissatisfied with the Terms of Service or experienced difficulties with their order: Authorize your customer support team to offer up to a certain amount to customers without your verbal approval. If your average sale is around $250, you can authorize customer support to offer customers up to $50 off their next order or a $20 cash refund. If the customer is still dissatisfied then the issue should be elevated to your attention for resolution.

THRESHOLD THEORY FOR
THE LIFESTYLE ENTREPRENEUR

The whole idea of Threshold Theory is to make concrete tangible progress on your business when you spend time working on it. It's about having something to show for the time you put into it as well as a placeholder that lets you jump back into your workflow at a later date without losing momentum. Rather, crossing thresholds builds momentum and acts as a ratchet does, propelling your ideas forward without the possibility of backsliding or losing focus.

You can always make changes later, but it's best to make changes after analyzing the product of your actions, than half-finished work that doesn't offer a clear basis for decision making.

Thresholds change across the three phases of entrepreneurship:

- Ideation: In the Ideation phase thresholds act as a means of turning your ideas into something tangible and queuing up possibilities to act on later after periods of reflection and inaction.
- Development to Launch: In the Development phase thresholds generally involve giving direction to service providers and constructively feeding back on their work.
- Launch and Growth: In the Launch and Growth phases you cross a threshold once it becomes clear that the marginal benefit of doing so exceeds the cost of continuing on with the status quo, but not before.
-

Thresholds are about increasing efficiency and accountability based on real world feedback and taking concrete steps to ensure that when you work on your business it is with the goal of making your business work for you.

Make Your Productivity Skyrocket
and Increase the Value of Your Time!
THE PRINCIPLE OF
THE POWER HOUR

"I always worked until I had something done and I always
stopped when I knew what was going to happen next.
That way I could be sure of going on the next day."

— Ernest Hemingway

Whether you're starting a new business, or operating an existing business in the mode of a Lifestyle Entrepreneur, Ernest Hemingway's advice on writing is spot on. One way to eliminate stress and decrease the amount of time spent on work is to take a task-based approach to workflow. This runs counter to the expectations of wage labor and salary-type work, but is in line with how many commissioned sales people work.

There is a lot of wasted productivity when people are expected to be at the office until a certain time even if there is no clearly defined objective to be accomplished. It is much better to step back into a workflow that you left after having accomplished a task and passed responsibility to someone else, and then they submit their work to you for review and further actions.

Most tasks associated with launching and growing an internet-based business can be fit into one-hour blocks of time or less. Blocking out a few hours a day, or every other day to focus intently on accomplishing well-defined objectives will help you make the most of that time, and consequently you'll start to value your time more and more as you become able to accomplish more in shorter intervals. This is a manageable and realistic commitment you can make to yourself that will help keep you focused and productive.

I had read about and experimented with many different productivity improvement techniques, but this point was really driven home when I was a university student. One semester I had classes ending at 10 a.m. and starting again at 11 a.m. on Monday, Wednesday and Friday. For that one hour break I would walk down to the computer lab and get as much done as possible work wise so I could focus on studying in the afternoons and evenings. As the semester went on I came to call that break "Power Hour", and once it became an institutionalized part of my weekly activities my productivity skyrocketed.

At any given time I've usually got 2-3 entrepreneurial projects on my plate and their requirements vary as each project progresses from Ideation and Development through to Launch and Growth. By way of example, that semester I was launching a nutritional supplements business, building the website infrastructure to release the first version of this book and redesigning my China-USA Traders website concurrently.

I pretty much stopped telling people all the projects I was working on because people either didn't believe I could be involved in three businesses with a 20 credit course load or they just thought I was bragging. But using the Principle of the Power Hour you can achieve the same levels of productivity or better!

How to Make The Most of Your Power Hour

In order to be most productive during a power hour, it is important to have your workflow set up so that you can jump right back in where you left off and execute decisions that will drive progress forward in your business. If you will be working with contractors on a talent platform like Elance.com then you simply need to log in and check up on the different projects that are ongoing. Providers will upload new designs or versions of a website to these workrooms and ask for your feedback or suggestions.

I will typically spend the first 15 minutes of a power hour quickly going over everything new that comes in. As a rule, I wait at least a few hours, and preferably a full day, before responding with my input and creative contributions. This is important because first impressions and knee-jerk reactions can often be misleading. For example, if I log on and see a new website design and my first reaction is "that sucks"; it is not necessary going to be helpful if I immediately write that to the provider. The prudent thing to do is to sit on it for a few hours, identify what exactly I don't like about it, and then write with pointed suggestions on what to change.

> As a rule, wait at least a few hours, and preferrably a full day, before responding with feedback and creative contributions.
>
> This is important because first impressions and knee-jerk reactions can often be misleading.

After going over everything new I'll pull up everything from earlier or the day before. Since I've been thinking about what I'm responding to for a few hours or more it is easy to quickly craft responses and fire off emails rapid fire.

The principle of the power hour functions best when you time-bridge your workflow like this; Reviewing work, designs, emails etc., and then going and doing something else let's your subconscious process what you've seen. Whether or not you are consciously thinking about it, the mind is at work and when you sit down to focus on work again the ideas and feedback come quickly.

After I've spent around 30 minutes responding to most or all of the open items on the agenda I'll spend the last 15 minutes of a power hour doing research and getting new ideas for the items I reviewed in the first 15 minutes. This helps stimulate new ideas and formulate responses to the new items on the agenda.

So if I'm reviewing new website designs in the beginning of the power hour, then in the last 15 minutes I'll look at relevant websites, read forums, and generally browse the web for material that will help me give the best feedback and suggestions for the provider to continue working.

Remember that working with power hours and time-bridging your workflow is most effective when you use Threshold Theory. When you are giving feedback to providers, answering emails or putting new jobs up for bid, your responsibility is to do enough so that the ball is put into someone else's court. This requires using clear, concise language when giving direction so there is little ambiguity about what you are expecting someone else to do.

Here is an example of the right and wrong way to give feedback to a designer. See if you can determine why the wrong way probably won't yield better results the next time, and why the right way should solve the problems.

Wrong Way to Communicate with Service Providers:

After reviewing the latest round of designs, something just doesn't feel right. I'm not sure what you were thinking with the brown and yellow color scheme on these homepage layouts, it just doesn't fit with this style of website. Can you try something different, maybe more professional and classy please? Also the menu bar doesn't seem to fit with the rest of the page. Can you change the colors, or maybe try a different style of lettering? Thanks.

Much Better Way to Get Quality Work:

After reviewing the latest round of designs I think we are making progress and there are just a few changes I'd like you to try. Instead of the brown and yellow color scheme, please use a dark red/maroon and muted orange, sort of like this: www.ReferenceWebsiteOne. com. Please create three variations with this color scheme using slightly different shades of colors so I can see what a few options will look like with this color scheme.

Also, for the menu bar, can you change the font of the text to be more like this site: www.ReferenceWebsiteTwo.com? Stylistically, I think the menu will look better if the buttons light up when the mouse is over the button. In the next round of designs, please show me two options of how a menu item lights up using a brighter shade of orange for one and a dark red for the other. Thanks and keep up the great work!

Do you see the difference between these two responses? The first one is ambiguous and slightly condescending. If I was the designer I wouldn't be inspired to do my best work with this kind of feedback. Adjectives like "classy" and "professional" are too open to interpretation to be useful and just saying "try a different style of lettering" doesn't give the designer a concrete suggestion of what to try instead.

> When working with online service providers communicating clearly and giving specific instructions save a lot of time and money.

Not only is a response like this unproductive, but it can be costly too. Without giving specific suggestions and reference sites the designer could spend hours trying ideas and you could still end up dissatisfied.

The second response is much better for a number of reasons; instead of questioning the designer's creative sensibilities, I say that we're making progress but there is still more to do. I give specific recommendations for a different color scheme and post a link to reference website that has a similar design. Then I ask for three variations using different shades of these colors. This only takes a short time for a designer since they are essentially just adjusting colors instead of going back to the drawing board and starting over.

For the menu suggestions, I give another reference website that uses the font I'd like them to try. Then I ask for two examples of how the menu could light up when the mouse rolls over a button and give two specific colors to try. The net result is that I will receive 3-5 design variations from this letter; three if the designer incorporates the menu suggestions into the same file as the color scheme variations, five if the two menu adjustments are incorporated into separate files.

Giving specific suggestions and referencing other websites saves time and money. Compare that with the first letter where it is hard to know what the designer will try or how long it will take for them to figure out what is meant by "classy" or "just doesn't feel right."

BLUEPRINT FOR A PRODUCTIVE POWER HOUR

It is not hard to accomplish a lot in one hour, provided you are working from the right blueprint. Here is an outline you can use, and of course feel free to try out variations and find a mix that works best for you:

- **15 Minutes** reviewing new work submitted by providers and scanning new emails. Write down your first impressions and feelings but don't send them. Spend just long enough to know the issues and consider a response.
- **30 Minutes** responding to providers and emails from earlier, making sure to cross thresholds and hand responsibility over to whoever is receiving your response. This should be a fast-moving process after having spent some time thinking through the best response and what your next round of feedback should consist of.
- **15 Minutes** browsing the web, researching reference sites and getting some initial ideas for how to craft the best responses to the new work and emails that have come in. For ongoing projects, try creating a bookmark folder in your web browser so you can easily store and access quality reference sites and content.

LIFESTYLE ENTREPRENEUR IN-FOCUS: ANDREW SMITH
First Class Flying and 5-Star Living Done In Style

When I think of successful Lifestyle Entrepreneurs, the one name that perpetually sits at the top of my list is Andrew Smith. Growing up in extremely adverse conditions, he has completely transcended them to become not only very wealthy, but is also an inspiration to others who regularly gives his time, energy and experience to help others develop and grow on their path to success. I was fortunate enough to pin him down in Munich, Germany earlier this year and interview him for your reading pleasure. Enjoy and prepare to be inspired:

<u>Jesse</u>: What were your circumstances growing up and how did your upbringing influence your desire to live the life you have now?

<u>Andrew</u>: I had a very normal childhood until I turned 10, then everything went dark and despite the best efforts of my mother it was very difficult. For a long time, I felt like little more than a leaf being blown around in the wind with little control or the ability to change my circumstances. I developed a degree of insecurity and a strong desire to stand out and prove myself too as a result. Money seemed to be at the heart of the family problems, or it seemed like the answer at least. I resolved to never experience those problems again.

Q: What was your first entrepreneurial venture, how did it end up, and what were the learning lessons you took away from it?

I started young. I was 5 years old and harassing the neighbors to buy homemade mint sauce on Sundays. That venture probably made me 50 pence but cost my parents five times as much. With my first real endeavor I jumped in at the deep end with a lot of naivety and little experience or understanding of business at 23. I signed a contract to open multiple health supplement stores in a chain of fitness centers without testing the concept. It ultimately failed and left me with a lot of debt and little wiggle room. I don't know of any successful people who haven't experienced a number of failures, so I think the greatest lesson I learned is that there's always going to be a certain amount of failing you have to do. How much I think is largely dependent on your work ethic, strength, upbringing, education, the people around you, and your ability to recognize the mistakes. More tangible would be to terminate failures fast and not to sign contracts without testing concepts first.

Q: Did you have mentors, advisors or inspirational people in your life that drove you towards entrepreneurship?

Not at the start, I had a wolf on my back that was ultimately my driving force and I always thought I had to paddle my own canoe, which meant never asking for help. Consequently success didn't come easily; in fact it was a very long on-ramp. Later on in life I found myself rising quickly through a network of people that worked together to pull each other up and I realized the power of

> **Money seemed to be at the heart of the family problems, or it seemed like the answer at least. I resolved to never experience those problems again.**

mentors. Now I regularly seek to connect and be connected to other like-minded people, together we throw ideas around, offer advice where relevant and discuss our experiences.

I think the greatest thing I've taken away from having mentors is to have mentors. It sounds simple but until I found myself surrounded by people who had been where I wanted to go, I didn't recognize the potential of that, nor did I realize how willing people are to offer up their hard won knowledge borne out of experience. My advice to anyone is to pick up the phone or write that email and ask people for help, and if they can't help, ask if they can put you in contact with someone who can. I've never had anyone say no.

Q: What is your business now and how is it structured?

My companies are largely structured on a fabric of technology. The system I have set up is heavily dependent on automation, outsourced labor and the Internet. To give some specifics, we have a number of websites, Amazon stores, and eBay stores retailing products, anything from cosmetics, to remote control helicopters, to cloud storage. From a consumer perspective, each website or store operates as a separate business, but the back end of each patches into the same Magento database.

From there we use readily available Magento plug-ins to parse data. We can do a lot with this information with very little or in many cases no human interaction. For example, as orders come in from our sales channels, the system creates a CSV file in real time and sends it to an order fulfillment warehouse company we use called The Fulfillment Station. They pick and pack the orders on our behalf, scan the tracking information and their system sends it back to ours. At this point our system will fire off customer service emails with the tracking information included. All of our orders are handled this way, including wholesale and distributor orders which come in through a private trade-only website.

> My companies are largely structured on a fabric of technology. The system I have set up is heavily dependent on automation, outsourced labor and the internet.

Our stock is managed in real-time, and crosschecked with the warehouse, again, using automated software. When we find ourselves running low on any item, an email is sent to me by the system with a stock report. Using algorithms we can take into account lead times and sales performance before these warnings are sent. From here I can create a purchase order with our manufacturers in China, the USA, or the UK. The stock is sent direct to the 3rd party order fulfillment warehouse so I never see it.

When we want to launch a new website, we have a 3rd party Magento developer create the front end using copy written by a copy writer we found on Elance.com, life-like images created by a 3rd party designer using 3d modeling software, and a web design created by a designer we found on 99designs.com. The developers then patch the new site into the same back end, the stock is ordered from manufacturers typically sourced on alibaba.com and delivered direct to the warehouse, who will have received notification in the form of a purchase order from the manufacturers. My team work together and I am kept in the loop but I'm largely free to steer the company and over-see projects. I can do this from wherever I want to be.

More traditional areas of the business are handled in a similar way. For example to receive mail, we use a mail forwarding company as our registered office address. They scan incoming mail and email me a copy. Our accountants can draw the sales reports direct from our website, and our manufacturers know to cc them into invoice emails. They are also cc'd into our email from the registered office address so get copies of our mail which includes bank statements, tax related documents, and invoices.

> The past year has been incredible. I've been fortunate enough to see my company's revenue grow by over 400% while living a life normally reserved for lottery winners.

Q: Give an overview for the last year of your life; Where did you travel, what were the highlights? What new inspiration or ideas did you uncover that you are putting into practice this year?

The past year has been incredible. I've been fortunate enough to see my company's revenue grow by over 400% while living a life normally reserved for lottery winners. I have lived in hotels almost the entire year and been handed the keys to the Presidential suite in more 5 star hotels than I can count. I took over 60 business class flights, visiting 39 cities in 20 countries across 5 continents.

I've played with and fed lions, taken a tiger cub for his morning exercise, swam with dolphins, scuba dived with sharks, shared a balcony with monkeys and flying lemurs overlooking one of the top 10 beaches in the world, spent a month snowboarding in Canada, and guest lectured at Oxford University. I took my mother and her partner to New York, rented a Lamborghini for an extended period of time, shared a private cabin with Angelina Jolie, the boy band Blue, and Jean Claude Van Damme on a flight to Bangkok, and most fulfilling of all helped change the lives of 12 men through a free transformational mentorship program I run every summer.

> It's not often you hit a half-court shot from the first throw of the ball, and it's not often you have immediate success in business. Growth happens over time, through constant evolution of the business.

People often assume that my life must be lonely but it's anything but. I've been lucky enough to spend time with some incredibly successful people, many of which shared their own success stories. I took away a number of ideas and strategies from these meetings, many of which are already being put into practice. For example we now have deals in place with many of the daily deals sites across the world, and we've recently began expanding our reach into social media through sponsorship and video production deals.

I not only got the ideas for both these expansion plans through the friends I made, but also the detailed blueprints or road maps for how to execute successfully, and the necessary contacts to do so efficiently and with ease.

Q: What is your advice to aspiring Lifestyle Entrepreneurs who want to build a business that can be run from anywhere in the world, allowing them to travel and explore their interests and passions in unique and creative ways?

Ask yourself what's stopping you from following your dreams. Rationalized fear is still fear. Don't be afraid of failure, I don't know who said it but I really like the phrase "there's no failure, just lessons". Let go of your pride if that's what stopping you.

So just start. You don't need a lot of money and regardless of your circumstance you can probably find the time.

People often think coming up with the initial idea is the hard part but it's not. The real work begins after you've found the first few sales. Its how do you create the ground swell that captures a greater audience. So I think it's important to have an understanding that it's rare to have much of an idea coming in of what's going to set you apart. It starts with an idea that you could make something work in an industry, but it's not until you get in it that you see where the angles can be played.

And iteration is equally as important. It's not often you hit a half-court shot from the first throw of the ball, and it's not often you have immediate success in business. Growth happens over time, through constant evolution of the business. Sometimes that means letting go of a strategy altogether, other times it means doing more of the same, ramping up over time.

Don't be afraid to leverage other people's money to effectuate growth. Organic growth sounds nice, but personally I think it's overrated as it stands to hold you back in many cases. There's an abundance of finance available through an equally numerous variety of lenders and money is currently cheap.

As for travel and lifestyle, my strongest advice would be to pick a hotel group and an airline within an alliance that best suits your needs and stay loyal. The benefits on offer for doing so make flying and hotel living very comfortable.

WHAT TYPE
OF BUSINESS
TO START?

Now, after a thorough introduction to some of the important concepts involved in being a Lifestyle Entrepreneur, we come to the critical question: What type of business to start? It is my hope that the ideas, concepts and exercises presented so far have stirred up a number of ideas and helped build a compelling case for you to design your own lifestyle.

The Discover Your Identity exercise from earlier is a useful tool to elicit your interests and passions as well as uncovering overlapping interests or untapped opportunities. It does not, however, tell you what type of business best suits your personality. That requires an inquiry into how you prefer to interact with people in a business context.

Some people are naturally charismatic and enjoy meeting and speaking with others face-to-face, where their personality can best be conveyed. Others value their privacy and autonomy, preferring instead to create the products and build the systems but to let others manage operations, or better, for the business to run itself.

During the research and drafting phase for this book I had a chance to reflect on all the businesses I've started across the years, and how different and seemingly unconnected they all are. There is not much overlap between being in a rock band, touring the US, dealing with promoters and running an indie record label, and building a custom USB flash drive business with operations in China, customer service in Pakistan and a design team in Kosovo and Argentina.

> It is helpful to begin with general principles and reasons before mapping out the specific actions and direction to take. We have covered the former, now let's dive into the details.

However, the common thread, which I finally have come to understand, is that collectively I have been fortunate enough to gain firsthand experience in all of the different types of business that I'm going to present to you!

But first...

GOING BACK TO THE START...
HARSH KRIEGER – LIVE IN ADRIAN, MICHIGAN

Standing in front of the church, talking to a potential investor, my most pressing thought was that we had $10,000 of salaries and marketing costs payable in the next 30 days, but only about $6,000 in the bank. And touring costs being incurred daily. Here we are at soundcheck for a charity event benefiting deaf people in Jamaica, who are apparently treated inhumanely. Within the open layout of the church with its wide bare walls, the sound swims through the pulpit, splashes off the alter, and washes over the pews like whitewater wrestling with each piece of corral in the Great Barrier Reef. Bombastic and full, I suppose we hoped for a big turnout to soak up some of the sound.

"You're playing a charity event at a church? In small-town Michigan? OK, what's after that," said the potential investor. I was stressed.

"Well, in fact we are also doing an autograph and photo session at the Meijer location here in Adrian tomorrow; they are carrying our record and helping get distribution in all 182 locations," I replied.

"That's cool, are you expecting a good turnout?"

"Definitely, this is Jake's home town and our first show here. It's a pretty tight knit community and there's not too much big news here, so they've been expecting us...which is fun. Plus we're selling merchandise and CDs tonight at the show."

"So how are you guys doing financially? What's your cash balance relative to your expenses?"

Being the one in charge of the bands finances and business, was taking its toll. We needed to continually raise money to finance the progression towards our album's official release on August 16, 2005. Four musicians living on the road with a tour manager costs about $250-300 a day, all in. Gas, food for five at Denny's, two rooms at a budget hotel and some drinks. Our manager, a hip black mother named Georgia, who lived in Staten Island, NY although we were based in Nashville, ran $2,000 a month, plus expenses. We were pushing our album to college radio and getting spins on around 300 stations, but the real killer was our commercial radio campaign and public relations which was close to $5,000 combined a month.

"Well, we have a considerable cash need leading up to and following our release date. Touring is expensive and radio and PR costs are high, but we're seeing results and building momentum." Maybe vague generalities will avoid telling him that we need his money or we're up shit creek without a paddle.

"My son has been taking guitar lessons, he practices to Harsh Krieger and asked his teacher to learn how to play Home so he could learn it." – Yes! His son is gonna close the deal. I make a mental note to send him an autographed poster.

"Oh yeah! That's so funny; you know I just sent an autographed poster made out to him with a special note. Hope he likes it!" I say mustering all the enthusiasm and boyish optimism I could muster.

"Ha ha, he'll love that." Ahhh we've finally bridged the gap from logical minded interrogation to rainbows and butterflies emotional rationalization – "OK, let's talk top of next week, maybe I can help you out with that $10,000."

Yes! I think, and breathe a sigh of relief.

"Sounds great, thanks! We're recording the show tonight, so I'll send you a copy," I say this time honestly relieved. Another bullet dodged. Everyone's getting paid this month.

I rejoin the guys inside and throw on my custom Telecaster with an original '59 pickup on the bridge. It's sharp piercing cry sounds like a hawk making a squealing nosedive into the Grand Canyon.

"Dude where were you? We gotta dial in your guitar tone so I can set up my ear mix," Jake said.

"I got caught up talking to a potential investor," I replied.

"Oh, that's cool. Dude are you going to wear the jacket tonight?"

"Nah, probably the Arlene's Grocery shirt. Leather jacket doesn't seem right in church."

"Nice, I'm gonna wear my CIA kitty abduction shirt," he says earnestly, referring to the shirt he sewed together a couple weeks ago.

And I laughed inside myself, relaxing somewhat for the first time in a few days. There comes a point where worrying about how to finance the band and our record label detracts from the experience of actually being in a band touring the country and releasing our album. I flirted with that line and did my best to keep any hesitation or self-doubt from spilling over to affecting the whole band. Sometimes I would try to put myself in Chris or Greg's shoes, our bassist and drummer respectively, to imagine what it would be like to be drawing a salary to tour and record all expenses paid. That's gotta be a pretty sweet gig at 21 years old.

Our role however, Jake and I, was to create the configuration that allowed others like Chris, Greg and our road manager Brett to step into; writing endlessly, recording the album, assembling a team, being selective about what shows to play, making ourselves available to media and, of course, picking up the tab. In the end I don't regret a thing. The steep learning curve exposed me to so much, so young, that the stress associated with managing people and expectations becomes an afterthought upon reflection.

With this thought in mind I came back to the present. We sound checked my guitar. First the baritone guitar with its long neck, wide spaced frets and fiberglass body. A thick syrupy sound springs forth with the help of a well-rosined cello bow and a foot-controlled delay pedal. I would tap the tempo of the song, or some subdivision thereof, with my foot while drawing the bow across the strings. With the bare cavernous walls of the church amplifying each delay I had visions of a thousand monks chanting "Ohhmmm".

Then the drums kick in and define the beat "wha-boom-boom-bam – wha-boom-boom-bam" and the rhythm guitar and bass drop. We're moving in sync, a sonic flood - now becomes a staccato groove. Jake's voice soaring above it all. We're locked in. And consequently all other thoughts are locked out.

Performing is an exercise in being present. The moment thoughts creep into your mind not relevant to what's happening on stage, the magic disappears. And being in the moment is such a beautiful thing.

We put down our instruments and head out to get a bite to eat with Jake's family. His parents are proud to have their son's big homecoming be announced in the press and, for a conservative Christian family, have come to embrace the fact that we all straighten our hair, wear tight jeans and sometimes mascara when performing.

Something playful and fun occurs when the image and attitude we adopt and project as a band collides with the dynamics and inside jokes of one of our families who have seen us go through numerous stages growing up. Like after Jake finished telling his mom about a TV performance we did on Good Day Alabama, beaming with pride – then her showing us a poem Jake wrote about kittens when he was in third grade.

And so a large part of touring is just life, in different cities. Pin points on a map with a yellow dashed line connecting them all. Staring out the window at the wide open fields and flatlands of America in shotgun, talking to Brett about what kind of bass rig Chris should get, while Jake and Greg sleep in the backseat. Driving from Nashville to Flagstaff in 34 hours straight while the world outside the windows stands still, while Oreo wrappers and Red Bull cans pile up throughout the van. Then cleaning up, warming up and rocking the house in downtown Phoenix not even a day later.

But now we're in Michigan and it's almost show time. The sun is setting across wide open fields of corn as we caravan back to the church. Now the lights are on and a swarm of people are congregated out front. The marquee read:

Performing Tonight: Harsh Krieger with special guest Alaris!

We go in the back and round up Jake's family and friends, which ends up being around 30 people, and bring them all back stage where there is catered food and beverages, plus some nice couches and TVs. The opening band is playing to a half full crowd in the 400 seat church auditorium but everyone is jumping around and enjoying it. I'm warming up on my Telecaster and enjoying talking to everyone who's known Jake since he was in first grade.

But really we're all thinking about playing. It is an all-consuming thought that creeps up starting a few hours before showtime, increasing in intensity up until the calm before the storm; walking up on stage, calm, cool and collected. Unaffected. Strap on your guitar with the stage lights off and ominous pre-recorded synthisizer music seeps from the PA, threatening at any moment to swell in intensity and explode into song.

Then I draw my bow across the strings and depress the delay pedal. The sound regenerates and expands, mixing in with the slightly off-key synthesizer. It swells and swells with each regeneration, in total darkness, the tension is palpable and thick. Then "da-boom-boom-beh – da-boom-boom-beh" and Greg comes in with the tom toms and kick while Chris drops the bass line and we're still all in darkness.

We cycle through one more time and crescendo – holding it – holding it: Deh-deh-deh deh-deh-deh bem bem: I switch off the delay, drop the bow and flick the pickup from bass to treble as the whole band comes in, exploding into movement as the bright yellow flood lights go on and sweep out across the crowd in an arc. Spotlights circle the stage as the intro plays then settle on Jake as we launch into the first verse of Gunsmoke: "Bang Bang Bang, breathing in Gunsmoke. Hey Hey Heeeey, before my lungs choke"

A sea of faces, with waving arms, sparkling in flashes when a light runs across them; Otherwise a dark abyss, the view from stage right behind my guitar rig spread around me in a semi-circle of functionality and possibility. Much like a palette from which to mix new colors from stalwart primary ingredients, audible Jackson Pollack splatters of sound. Spit forth from the speakers in staccato resonant bursts. Dancing with the vocal melody, an all-consuming call and response accompanied by complementary motions, tossing our hair wildly for emphasis at the right times. Staggering movements and explosive drum and bass carry the song.

Jake's singing. I'm playing. We're in Adrian, Michigan on a Friday night and the whole town is out to see their hometown hero's triumphant return to trapped-in-time Adrian. It's so fun to get caught up in the moment. Suddenly I don't care how our album is doing at radio in Little Rock, Arkansas, and I don't care if our manufacturer got the check our manager sent last week on time. I'm not a bean counter or a manager.

This is my way of contributing to the world right now in my life, using music's sweet melodious majesty to bequeath joy unto the faithful friends and family gathered in this church tonight. We're not a Christian band, but generally we're all Christian guys, and the spirit of giving is alive in the hearts of Michigan's Christians, who have worked so hard to bring us to Adrian to support the deaf people of Jamaica by way of raising funds for their mission work. Well God bless them, let's make them proud.

So the show that I thought would be a lackluster evening in the boonies on our way to Grand Rapids, turned out to be quite profound. We played with the audience, as in, we interacted so much. The inspirations for several of Jake's lyrics stood scattered through the crowd, receiving his smiling acknowledgement at the right time,

"Well it's deeper than all the oceans combined, and it's stronger than the change. The change of time. You change your mind."

Some people here knew what I was going to play next, so I played into it and slid up to the edge of the stage before guitar breaks tossing my hair back and forth smiling while wailing with my back arched and the neck of my Telecaster aiming to shoot out the lights.

"Does anybody else feel me now? I feel cold, old and all left out. Yeah, tired and wasted on all these dreams that we believed and dreamed."

I see Brett up in the sound booth some thirty feet above the crowd bobbing his head. We're recording the show and he's got his hands full but doing a great job with our on-stage mixes. It is just the best when everything sounds right on stage, and it's surprisingly hard to make it so. Brett's toured with Lonestar and has a platinum record on his wall, but he's here with us too in Adrian, Michigan having more fun than we expected to have.

"Dreamed our hearts away. Dreamed it every day."

Chris and Greg are playing facing each other and Jake does a Chuck Berry like stagger towards me, then I counter and drive him back towards the center of stage, pushing and pulling back and forth upon the iridescent marionette strings that synchronize our fingers along each of our respective guitar necks.

"Holy Moses, it goes like this – put your hopes in, hope to get them back again."

Jake thanks, by name, each of the people who have helped us make this evening possible, and makes a point of noting that we've all come together to help people in need. He also thanks the manager of the Meijer's store in Adrian where we did an autograph signing earlier.

"Lessons way up in the night sky, waiting for the right time"

Now it's our last song and I wish we had a longer set. We play a new song called Grounded, with its epic soundscape chorus. I wave my arm back and forth over my head, looking out encouragingly into the crowd's hidden abyss. Then lights flash over the crowd and there is a sea of swaying arms waving right back at me.

May 2005
Adrian, Michigan
USA

What's Your Type?
STARTING THE BUSINESS
THAT'S RIGHT FOR YOU

From a young age up until the time when I got serious about music as a career I didn't give too much concern to the different types of businesses out there. The circumstances of being in a band and wanting to retain creative control dictated that starting our own record label was the natural choice. At the time, not thinking of it from a strategic macro-economic perspective, I just charged right in. This was at a time when compact discs (CDs) sales were falling 20% per year as downloads and piracy were running rampant, and it was becoming a bigger and bigger deal to "go platinum" and sell 1,000,000 records. None of those things deterred me from building a business plan around selling CDs and touring.

> Always focus on playing to your strengths instead of always strengthening your weaknesses
>
> Build a team of advisors to help you in areas that you are weak and round out your strengths

I built a team of advisors who graciously helped me get my MBA first-hand, in the School of Life. Anytime I didn't know something about how to structure a contract or compensate employees I could call one of them and get the answer in short order. These mentors, while not involved in the day-to-day operations of our band or record label, were very helpful in the sense that they gave me the confidence to try things I was uncertain of. Once we recorded a three song demo and began playing shows in the surrounding towns, we realized how much it would actually cost to produce and release an album nationwide. After talking with our advisors for a few months, many of them agreed to lend us the money to help realize our vision.

It felt great to have no formal education past high school but still be able to start a record label, get a team of advisors and ultimately raise enough money to record our album and promote it all across America. In hindsight it was a learning experience where I discovered many of the ideas in this book first hand, through lots of trial and error. Running a label, and being the band was a unique experience; like being both the salesman and the product. The highs felt higher knowing that it was a result of hard work paying off, but the lows were brutal since getting a bad review for a show or an album felt like a personal attack as well as a business problem.

Fast forward to today and I am now very conscious of the dynamics of each business I start or partner in. Being the sales person and the product can quickly become an all-encompassing proposition when you want to scale your business. For a Lifestyle Entrepreneur type of business, it may be preferable to completely divorce business operations from your personality and identity.

In this section I'd like to introduce a chart that maps what I consider to be the four different types of business:

THE FOUR TYPES OF LIFESTYLE ENTREPRENEUR BUSINESSES

TYPE 1 **Online - Custom** Custom offering of product or service transacted online	TYPE 2 **Online - Standard** Identical physical or digital products transacted online
TYPE 3 **Offline - Custom** Custom tailored product or service delivered in person	TYPE 4 **Offline - Standard** Similar products and services delivered in person

BUILD YOUR BUSINESS BASED ON YOUR LIFESTYLE GOALS

Matching Your Type to Your Identity

As you have probably guessed by now, the point of this book is for you to envision the perfect lifestyle and determine how much it would actually cost to live it. Then, and only then, should you design a business to put a financial foundation under your castle in the clouds; to finance your lifestyle and creative constructs.

When it comes to starting a Lifestyle Entrepreneur style business, it is important to make sure you start the type of business that is right for you. Let's take a look at the four primary ways that products and services are offered and delivered to customers, as well as Vision-MAPs for each type based on my previous businesses. See which one resonates most with your personality.

TYPE 1	TYPE 2
Online - Custom	**Online - Standard**

TYPE 3	TYPE 4
Offline - Custom	**Offline - Standard**

Lifestyle Entrepreneur Business
TYPE 1: ONLINE - CUSTOM

This type of business provides a general type of good or service but allows for the customer to personalize some aspect of it. Customers can inform themselves online, see options for custom tailoring and ultimately purchase a personalized product or service from the website. As a Lifestyle Entrepreneur Type 1 businesses can take longer to set up than a standardized Type 2 or 4 business, but the customization option allows for higher margins and a broader base of customers than may purchase standardized offerings.

Examples of Type 1 businesses are bespoke fashion, customizable products like the popular Build-A-Bear Workshop, and online coupon sites where users create custom profiles and receive offers tailored to their interest. Once the business architecture is in place, high-growth can be achieved as customers define the product mix that works best for them and tell their friends.

Type 1 Business Pros: Customization can create a broad customer base that is loyal due to their personal connection to the business or brand. Revenue model can adapt to customer preferences easier than a standardized offering.

Type 1 Business Cons: Longer set-up time and management requirements than a standardized offering. Can be programming-intensive and require ongoing support from a development team if you are not a programmer.

The following Vision-MAP of my former business Village Green Energy outlines a template for this type of business. In this case, we built a carbon calculator to determine the customer's environmental impact and then offered customizable options to offset that impact. Customers could choose from a selection of solar power, wind turbines and biogas generators to power their home or business. This connected concerned citizens with a customizable way to live a green, sustainable lifestyle.

Vision-MAP for Village Green Energy

After working on clean energy projects as an investment banker, I co-founded a company called Village Green Energy (VGE) to work directly in the carbon credit and compliance market. VGE purchases clean energy credits from solar, wind and biogas energy generators and sells them retail to businesses and households who want to reduce their carbon footprint. We also built a Facebook application which addressed sustainability in the wine industry. The company was sold in 2010.

Vision: Provide a realistic way for concerned businesses and individuals to reduce their carbon footprint and communicate their efforts with customers, friends and family.

Mission: Build a portfolio of renewable energy generators to sell VGE wholesale energy credits. Build a network of businesses and customers to purchase retail energy credits.

Actions: Design VGE Renewable Energy Certificates. Build Facebook application to connect wine lovers with environmentally conscious wineries. Negotiate with landlords to include energy credits in their lease agreements with tenants. Partner with municipalities and townships to source electricity from renewable sources.

Product: Work within California energy compliance market to increase development of renewable energy sources. Leverage Facebook community to generate awareness and sales. Track aggregate environmental impact through carbon calculator.

Selected Accomplishments:

- Awarded Green Power Partnership by U.S. Environmental Protection Agency.
- Generate over $30,000 of energy credit sales in two weeks via Facebook app.
- Offset millions of pounds of CO_2 from entering the atmosphere.
- Sold company to a clean energy investor in 2010.Lifestyle Entrepreneur Business

Lifestyle Entrepreneur Business
TYPE 2: ONLINE - STANDARD

This type of business sells one type of product online, usually in a set format with few if any variations. Customers generally have access to all the information they need to make a purchasing decision online and incentives to buy such as bonus products or a satisfaction guarantee. If there are options to personalize the product, it is usually minor and cosmetic in nature, such as a different color of the same product or the printing of a company logo.

Examples of Type 2 businesses are eBooks and information products, single-product feature companies (think late-night infomercials) and wholesale products that are re-purchased frequently like flash drives that businesses give away at conferences and trade shows. The advantage of Type 2 businesses is that once you set up the architecture and have a process for fulfilling orders in place; it is possible to remove yourself completely from day-to-day operations.

Type 2 Business Pros: Good for Lifestyle Entrepreneurs that plan on travelling abroad and not necessarily being on a computer or working every day. Of course it takes some time and energy to set up the business, but once you know the costs for marketing in order to get enough customers to support your lifestyle, it is possible to decrease your involvement to a few hours a week.

Type 2 Business Cons: Bad for those who enjoy working closely with clients and colleagues in person. This is a business type that can scale the sales of a single product or limited selection of products, but is far removed from a close working relationship with clients, like what you would find consulting or in physical retail.

Following is a Vision-MAP for my former company USB Superstore which was mostly a Type 2 business, although we entertained some Type 1 clients who were willing to pay big money for customized services.

Vision-MAP for USB Superstore

My first attempt at building a fully-automated Lifestyle Entrepreneur business was USB Superstore. We sold custom f lash drives in wholesale quantities. Our manufacturers in China would send finished product directly to customers in boxes with USB Superstore on all sides, so we never carried an inventory or directly handled the product. This allowed me to run the business from anywhere with an Internet connection. I sold the business in early 2010.

Vision: Build a business that can be run from anywhere in the world using a laptop and Internet connection.

Mission: Become a trusted provider of wholesale custom USB flash drives. Build a global team of service providers that can be managed online.

Actions: Structure service level agreements with factories in China. Engage a sourcing agent to manage quality of orders in China. Set incentives for sales executives and train customer service representatives. Negotiate business development deals to expand into new markets. Create training materials and delegate responsibilities to managers to remove myself from operations.

Product: Receive repeat business from satisfied customers. Receive increasingly better terms from factories based on overall quantities ordered. Customer referrals as a source of new revenue. High rankings in search engines as a result of online marketing efforts. Manage multiple teams through Elance.com and other online platforms.

Selected Accomplishments:

- $500,000 business in first operating year
- #1 search result on Google for "Wholesale USB" and other valuable terms.
- Clients include Harvard Business School, BMW, Audi and United Nations.
- Company sold to private investors in 2010, business still operational today.

Lifestyle Entrepreneur Business
TYPE 3: OFFLINE - CUSTOM

This type of business delivers a highly personalized experience to the client and involves a great deal of personal attention from the Lifestyle Entrepreneur. Clients generally speak with the company at length about their needs and resources before entering into a contract. However, since the business is so relationship-based, acquiring one or two clients can easily provide enough income to finance an enjoyable lifestyle. The nature of Type 3 businesses are generally long-term engagements with clients such as consulting and advisory services or customized coding and software development work.

Examples of Type 3 businesses are consultancies, accounting & book keeping, investment banking, website and software developers and custom engineering firms. All of these businesses tailor their work to the needs of the client and generally work closely over the course of contract. The price you can command is highly correlated to the skills, expertise and relationships you have in the field of interest.

Type 3 Business Pros: High pay for developed skills and strong relationships. Good for team players who enjoy working closely with clients and colleagues.

Type 3 Business Cons: Difficult to maintain a work-life balance if your lifestyle goals involve lots of travel. Not ideal for introverts who would rather work behind the scenes than directly with clients.

Following is a Vision-MAP for what started as Krieger Consulting Group and eventually became a Vice President position at a boutique investment bank specializing in small-cap stocks and high-growth companies.

Vision-MAP for Consulting & Investment Banking

Earlier in the book I described how the consulting firm I launched, Krieger Consulting Group, grew our client base and connected them with investors. Eventually I merged that business into a California-based investment bank and assumed the title of Vice President of Investment Banking. The deal was structured so I could work remotely and deal directly with the CEO on all deals. This allowed me broad operating leeway to pursue lifestyle goals, while still being able to marshal the resources of an organization to help close business.

Vision: Work autonomously as an investment banker, sourcing deals from around the world and leveraging a registered broker-dealer when needed.

Mission: Merge consulting firm with investment bank in exchange for title of Vice President of Investment Banking. Build a network of CEOs, investors and entrepreneurs to participate in multiple deals.

Actions: Study and pass the Series 7 & 63 securities licenses. Structure investment opportunities with client companies and communicate them to investors. Negotiate terms sheets and structure deals. Advise clients on investment and divestment strategies. Facilitate business development opportunities for client companies.

Product: Take companies public via reverse merger. Raise additional money based on prevailing share price. Provide financing for high-growth tech, alternative energy and consumer products companies. Manage client expectations and provide ongoing guidance.

Selected Accomplishments:

- Raised over $1,000,000 in retail investments into high-growth tech company.
- Negotiate terms sheets and manage investments worth over $20,000,000.
- Meet with Jamaica's Minister of Energy & Commerce for an ethanol project.
- Get to drive $100,000 company car for being a top performer (BMW 645ci).

Lifestyle Entrepreneur Business
TYPE 4: OFFLINE - STANDARD

This type of business delivers a consistent product or service to customers in an offline environment. Customers can inform themselves online and decide if what is offered is right for them, but once they make a purchasing decision, the experience is consistent from one customer to the next. Type 4 businesses can be found in a wide variety of industries. Whether it is monthly delivery of nutritional supplements or a rock band playing shows, selling CDs and licensing songs to TV and film, the offering is consistent from one customer to the next.

Type 4 businesses can scale easily if the revenue model is subscription-based or involves selling a low-to-mid priced product to a broad base of customers. It can be difficult to scale if the Lifestyle Entrepreneur is also "the product" such as in a band scenario, or delivering seminars and workshops in different cities. The upshot is that if demand increases for Type 4 service businesses, you can always raise your rates instead of taking on more and more work.

Type 4 Business Pros: Can be scaled rapidly for physical products, or command high prices for in-person services. In-person training, consulting or performances can facilitate travel experiences, which can blend well with Creative Constructs and lifestyle preferences.

Type 4 Business Cons: Can require logistical and managerial support to scale; harder to be a one-person business for in-person services. It can be expensive to build market share for physical products if heavy advertising is required.

Following is the Vision-MAP for my first experience as a Lifestyle Entrepreneur, my former band Harsh Krieger. The revenue model combined physical product sales with live performances and licensing.

Vision-MAP for Harsh Krieger & Tabula Rasa Records

Harsh Krieger, my former band, was truly the beginning of my journey as a Lifestyle Entrepreneur. In fact, prior to having that experience I had practically zero interest in business. It was only the desire to fully realize my/our potential as musicians that drove me to learn about business from the ground up. So at the age of 21 my band mate Jake Harsh and I incorporated an independent record label called Tabula Rasa Records and signed ourselves as the first act on the roster. Looking back on the experience through the filter of the Vision-MAP framework, we can classify it like this:

Vision: Be professional musicians on our own terms, retain creative control and chart our own course in the industry.

Mission: Form an independent record label. Raise money to produce, release and market album. Tour America to support album. Touch lives with our songs and stories.

Actions: Hire manager to administer day-to-day affairs. Hire booking agents to negotiate with promoters and book tours. Coordinate producer, studio musicians, recording, mixing and mastering engineers to produce album. Manage radio and video promotions to support album launch. Reach out to music directors for licensing opportunities on TV shows.

Product: Monitor cash flow against budget. Compare SoundScan numbers with radio play markets. Interact with fans and solicit ideas. Ensure band and team operating sustainably.

Selected Accomplishments:

- First single "Home" peaked at #1 on MediaGuide's Independent Rock Chart.
- Airplay for "Home" music video on over 25 video outlets including MTV.
- Nine songs appear on MTV's Real World and Road Rules.
- Two nation-wide tours of America in 2005.

LIFESTYLE ENTREPRENEUR IN-FOCUS: JASPER RIBBERS
The Traveling Dutchman

Staring out across the French Alps, strapped into a snowmobile with wings, the roar of the engine drowned out any second thoughts or last minute hesitations. Revving the throttle and dropping into it into gear, the snow bank started to fall away and at last dropped out of sight while the peaks across the valley towered up into the sky. As he picked up speed, Jasper kept his eyes on the drop off and steadied his hands. Then just as the snow bank dipped out of sight he gunned the engine and aimed the nose up catching the wind underneath the hang glider-like wings. As he climbed up over the long glacial valley a smile crossed his face knowing that he could check off another item on the bucket list later on, assuming he could land this thing.

> So at age 32 he quit his lucrative but stifling corporate job to become a "full time citizen of the world."

Now about halfway through a long list of amazing adventures, all of which seemed totally unrealistic when writing them, Jasper is living his dreams every day. Growing up in the Dutch city of Arnhem, "my parents always stressed the importance of looking outside the Netherlands for opportunities and were pleased to see my curiosity in other countries, languages and cultures," he said. Looking for a way to leverage this interest into an online business, Jasper and a few friends and got together and "we started a Dutch poker website, which soon expanded to include English, Spanish, German, Italian and Russian languages and players. As the business grew it put a strain on our relationship and I realized how important it is to not let business disagreements effect personal relationships," he said.

Even though he didn't know many entrepreneurs growing up, Jasper was determined to find a way to live on his own terms and not end up working hard his whole life just to end up "perched atop a pile of assets, with my youth and energy gone". So at age 32 he quit his lucrative but stifling corporate job to become a "full time citizen of the world." After studying search engine optimization (SEO) and web design in his spare time for over a year, Jasper set out to build a number of online business he could run from anywhere in the world from his laptop.

"I remember the summers of my childhood as wonderfully blissful times. I played in the forest with my friends, ate ice cream at the corner store when it got too hot, kicked a football around in the park with my brothers, and then climbed trees with my girlfriend until the sunset. My life was directed solely by my fleeting desires.

How perfect. This is what I sought again, and this is why I broke away from the corporate rat race. I wanted to do what I wanted to do, go where I wanted to go, and spend time with whomever I wanted to spend time with," he said.

With that vision firmly held in his mind, Jasper quit his job and listed his apartment in Holland on AirBnB.com to start funding his initial travels. While still helping run the poker website, he said, "I decided to launch an online nutritional supplement business together with my partner who takes care of the production and distribution. This allows me to be location independent." The business consists of an online web store with a number of popular nutritional supplements. On the back-end there are agreements with companies to "drop-ship" orders to the end customer, so there is no need for inventory on hand. Taking advantage of the SEO skills gained from studying at night after his former job, Jasper was able to get the website ranked highly for a number of popular search terms, sending a steady stream of customers to their site every day.

> "I wanted to do what I wanted to do, go where I wanted to go, and spend time with whomever I wanted to spend time with."

With a few online businesses up and running and his apartment in Holland making money on AirBnB, Jasper managed to visit 13 countries last year! "I started off celebrating NYE in Bangkok, went surfing and diving in the Philippines, hiked the great wall in China, went skiing in Austria, skydiving in Hungary, and visited friends in New York, Los Angeles, San Francisco, San Diego, Shanghai, Beijing, Hong Kong and Tokyo and partied in Vegas, Amsterdam, Montreal, Budapest and Stockholm," he said.

Somewhere in between China and Europe, Jasper swung through San Francisco and he told me about his latest project.

"After reading Lifestyle Entrepreneur and doing the discover your identity exercise, it just hit me, I need to start a blog with my bucket list and stories from checking them off one-by-one."

And so TheTravelingDutchman.com was born!

Now with an outlet to share videos of him flying snowmobiles in the Alps and diving with whale sharks in the Philippines, Jasper is focusing on making the most of every day and sharing adventures with friends. But he still found time to share some sage advice for aspiring Lifestyle Entrepreneurs around the world:

"I think the most important factors in creating a successful online business are to do something that you love and have affinity with. Choose a niche focus where you can make an impact as a new entrant and identify your competitive advantage. Make this your focus and outsource the rest. Make your business your main focus in life for a while and put in as much work as possible, then once it's working for you, go out and do everything your heart desires."

Getting

Down to

Business

with

THE
OPERATIONS
MODEL

"If you have built castles in the air, your work need not be lost; that is where they should be. Now put the foundations under them."

— Henry David Thoreau

We have covered a lot of ground in the first sections of this book. From discovering your identity to designing a dream lifestyle to examining deep-rooted beliefs and creating a Vision-MAP, I hope you have gained a new perspective on life and how it can be lived with passion and purpose. Now it is time to get down to business and look at the details of building a business to support your lifestyle and fund your Creative Constructs.

To that extent I would like to present The Operations Model. This is an online business architecture that lets you bring your Lifestyle Entrepreneur business to life. Whether you want a business that runs on its own, or to personally interact with all your clients, The Operations Model outlines the process for finding customers, delivering your product or service and maintaining your customer base over time.

Once you have decided what type of business to start and defined the product or service you'll offer, The Operations Model outlines the path from prospective customer, to paying customer, to repeat customer. With a little practice most of the operational functions of a business can be systematized and outsourced, leaving you with more free time to focus on your passions and build new creative constructs.

After looking at The Operations Model as a whole, we'll look at each component in detail and I'll share my tips and tricks to make your business run like a well-oiled machine. So let's get started!

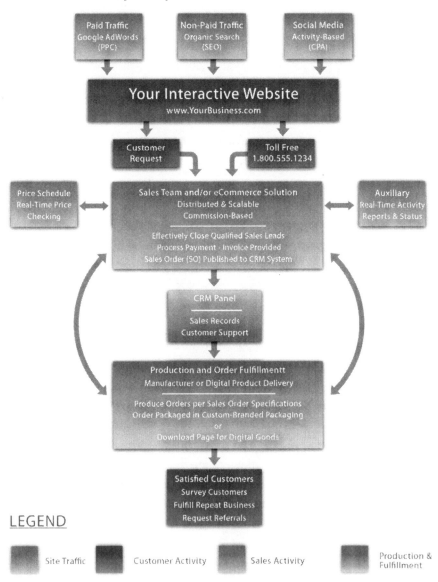

THE OPERATIONS MODEL
Lifestyle Entrepreneur Online Business Architecture

START THE ENGINE OF YOUR
LIFESTYLE ENTREPRENEUR BUSINESS!
An Overview of The Operations Model

The Operations Model describes a lean business architecture that does not require an office, a staff or much overhead beyond website hosting. It is the distillation of everything necessary to generate sales and make money on an order-by-order basis. Once you've got the systems in place and understand how to process one order through The Model, you can process a thousand. Of course, each customer has their own unique circumstances, but the process remains largely the same. As more activity takes place, you have more information to refine the processes that power it. In this sense, the business becomes more efficient the longer it operates; a virtuous cycle.

In many respects, using this business model is the smart way to do business these days. There's no need to establish your own design, engineering and manufacturing capabilities – a daunting proposition to say the least. Instead, you have a portfolio of production and fulfillment facilities or online e-commerce software to fulfill orders on your behalf. All you have to do is determine a product or service that can add value to customers in your target market, and then tailor the components of The Operations Model to fit your purposes.

The remainder of this book will focus on understanding The Model and the perspectives of the Owner, the Customers and the Operators. Each constituent's experience and expectations of the business are different, and it is important to optimize the business to accommodate each one's needs as best as possible.

When everyone's needs are met, you will be making money with as little stress and operating friction as possible.

Generally we will assume the following about each:

1. **The Owner** wants a business that maximizes profit and minimizes risk while providing customers with products that they want at a competitive price.
2. **The Customers** want quality products at competitive prices and the option to speak with someone knowledgeable and courteous when needed.
3. **The Operators** want to work on reliable systems, be compensated equitably in a timely manner and not have to deal with bureaucracy.

The Model is a virtual architecture for your Lifestyle Entrepreneur business and every component of The Model represents a function that needs to be executed by either:

- **The Owner** – You! Learning how to operate the basic functions of each component is important, if only so you can delegate to:
- **The Operators** - Your team of contractors sourced through online talent platforms or in-house salaried employees

For some individuals, the goal is to put the entire operation on "auto pilot" where every function the business performs is handled by external service providers who work as independent contractors. Others like to be more hands-on, staying involved in the day-to-day operations and personally executing the functions needed to run the business. Either way it is a good practice to learn at least the basics of each function in The Model, if only to be a more effective delegator later.

Now let's take a look at The Model, as experienced from the customer's perspective. My former business, www.USBsuperstore.com, is a real business built using The Model as a template for its business architecture. The customer is a composite character that represents a real segment of customers in the USB industry. As you read through the case study, try to put yourself in the customer's shoes and visualize the process from this perspective. See if you notice each component of The Model at work underneath the narrative.

UNDERSTANDING THE MODEL THROUGH A CUSTOMER'S EXPERIENCE
Buying Custom USB Flash Drives Online

Jonathan is the marketing director of TechCo, a technology products company. He regularly attends conferences and exhibitions as a representative for his company. This year, Jonathan decided to set his company apart from his competitors at the annual industry conference. Instead of handing out the usual logo pens and a folder full of marketing materials, he wanted to give away customized flash drives preloaded with a free trial of their new software to every attendee that provided him with their email address and phone number.

Looking on Google, he did a couple of searches, using terms like "custom flash drives" and "wholesale USB drives." He noticed one company on the first page of the search results page for a number of searches, who was also advertising on the right-hand side of the search results page. So he clicked through to the www.USBsuperstore.com website.

After looking through the website and reading about the products and services offered, he submitted a Quotation Request that described what he was looking for and

> **He noticed one company on the first page of the search results for a number of searches...so he clicked!**

included a note about which product style he thought would look good with TechCo's logo.

Within an hour, Jonathan received a phone call from a USBsuperstore.com sales representative who seemed to understand just what he wanted and was both knowledgeable and courteous. The sales epresentative made a couple of additional recommendations based on the colors of TechCo's logo and then emailed him a customized graphic mock-up of the drives with the logo in place and a cost.

Jonathan took the concepts to his boss who was both impressed with the idea and Jonathan's initiative. After going over a few more details, his boss approved the order. Jonathan called the sales representative back and placed the order, paying for it with the company credit card right over the phone.

Later that same day an email arrived with a confirmation of the order and the invoice marked 'paid'. The sales representative also requested the graphics files needed to print the logo on the drives. Jonathan sent the information and received a confirmation email that the files were received and the order went into production.

On the customer's side, the job was done. All he had to do was await the notification that the shipment was on its way with a tracking number.

With the sale closed and the necessary files in hand, the production process could begin. The sales representative created a new Sales Order in the USBsuperstore.com customer relationship management (CMS) system and titled it: TechCo-101. The sales representative then informed the Production Team to start the fulfillment process, referencing the files and production information included in the Sales Order.

A Production Team representative confirms that order TechCo-101 was received and that she would contact the sales representative if there were any questions about the order while it was being produced. Since everything needed was included in the Sales Order, the production team determined the total cost of the order and the estimated delivery time.

With these two pieces of key information the Production Team created a new Purchase Order within the CRM titled TechCo-101, so correspondence on the order matched the identifier used on the Sales Order. The Purchase Order contained the actual manufacturing costs for the drives that Jonathan ordered as well as the expected delivery date.

Once the order was manufactured, the Manufacturing Team shipped the drives to Jonathan at TechCo in USBsuperstore.com-branded packaging and published the tracking number to the Purchase Order titled TechCo-101.

At this point, the sales representative wrote Jonathan back informing him that the drives had been shipped and provided the tracking number for the shipment. The drives arrived and were a huge hit at the trade show. Customers loved the fact that they got a free trial of TechCo's new software on a flash drive that they could use for storing other data as well.

A week after the trade show, the sales representative sent a follow-up to see if Jonathan was satisfied and offered a $35 discount on his next order if he would take a few minutes to fill out a short customer satisfaction survey.

Three months later, Jonathan placed a larger order for the same style of drives. Since USBsuperstore.com already had his information on file, all that was needed was to process his payment and produce the order!

LOOKING UNDER THE HOOD OF THE OPERATIONS MODEL
Site Traffic: Enticing Potential Customers to Your Online Storefront

Note in the previous narrative that the first thing Jonathan did was some initial research by entering search words and phrases into a search engine. It may seem obvious, but it's important to see that the USBsuperstore.com made it a very high priority to be visible in all of the major search engines for a wide range of industry and product-specific search terms.

This is why the company was visible in the organic search engine results page (SERP) for different terms or words. This process is known as search engine optimization or SEO. This is a process whereby keywords and search phrases relevant to the business are woven through the site content and coding of the website in specific ways to boost visibility for those terms.

To further support their legitimacy as a vendor, they also advertised through Google's AdWords platform using many of the same search terms. AdWords is Google's advertising platform that places ads on the right side of the SERPs. AdWords has lots of helpful tools to help you identify the best search words to help you advertise your products and services so they can reach the right customers. These are helpful whether you're aiming for a broad target audience or a very narrow one. It is also one of the most efficient ways for you to bring prequalified customers to your site, since they see your advertisement at the exact time that they are thinking about products in your industry.

As an AdWords advertiser, you pay per click, which means you only pay when someone clicks on your ad. This is known as pay per click advertising, or PPC for short.

Social media traffic, or referral traffic, which are links from other sites to the USBsuperstore.com site, are another way to find potential customers. These links can either be part of an article published in a knowledge database, or they can be part of an affiliate campaign whereby others drive qualified traffic to your site in exchange for compensation. Generally for affiliates, you pay the affiliate a set fee once the visitor completes a specific task, such as submitting a Quotation Request or signing up for your newsletter. This type of advertising is known as cost-per-action, or CPA.

The key here is that because USBsuperstore.com has a solid SEO and PPC strategy in place, they were able to draw Jonathan to their site, even though he didn't have any prior knowledge of their existence. It's akin to offline advertising insofar as an advertiser for, say, plumbing goods would take out a billboard ad across the street from a hardware store.

Calls to Action on Your Website
Converting a Visitor to a Qualified Sales Lead

When it comes to searching for products on the Internet, people generally have a short attention span and a low tolerance for poorly designed, non-intuitive websites. So it's vital that your website:

- **Is easy to find through SEO and PPC.**
- **Grabs their attention and prominently displays calls to action.**

It's also important to feature a limited number of products that are highly visible (preferably on the homepage). If you overwhelm them with information and decisions, they will just suffer from *paralysis by analysis* and likely not make a decision at all, except to leave your site.

By focusing on a small selection of popular featured items, USBsuperstore effectively convinced Jonathan to submit a Quotation Request (one of the Calls to Action), which described, to the USBsuperstore, exactly what he was looking to purchase. Sure, there is an option on the site to view a full selection of products, but about 80% of the time the Quotation Requests submitted cite one of the three products featured on the homepage.

So for USBsuperstore.com, the first call to action is to submit a Quotation Request. This is a quick web form that collects a prospective customer's name, email address, phone number, as well as the product style, quantity and memory size of flash drive they are considering. Once the request is sent, the prospective customer gets a thank you message with a promise to follow-up on the query and the Sales Team receives the quotation request via email.

The other call to action available on the site is a toll-free phone number so the prospect can speak directly with a sales representative. When the prospect calls the toll free number, an Interactive Voice Response (IVR) system greets him or her, routing the call to the right department or person. **It may go something like this:**

> *"Welcome to the USB Superstore, the one-stop shop for all your custom USB flash drive needs. For Sales, Press 1…"*

In contrast to just a few years ago, when an IVR required physical hardware and cost thousands of dollars, today a professional quality IVR can cost as low as $9.95/mo. and can be set up online with no hardware whatsoever. It only takes about 15-30 minutes to subscribe to an IVR service, set up a voice menu of options, and enter numbers to forward the call to based on those choices. This includes getting your own toll-free number as part of the service.

In many cases, you can type the script that the listener will hear directly into the IVR along with the numbers to route calls to. If no one is available, the caller can leave a message, which is then sent as an mp3 audio file, via email, to the appropriate person. The recipient can listen to the audio file right from their workstation and call back when time permits.

> USB Superstore has two clear calls-to-action on their homepage:
>
> 1) Submit a quote request
>
> 2) Call a toll-free number
>
> The primary focus is to drive sales

Although we've all had at least one frustrating call center experience, they are very efficient from a business owner's perspective and can be very clear and succinct. The goal here is not to give potential customers the runaround via automated voice menus, but rather to get them in touch with the Sales Team as quickly as possible. Having a toll-free number and an IVR lends an aura of legitimacy to your business, even if the calls are being routed to your home phone line in the early stages.

Taking it a step further, new concepts are even getting rid of the menu options or even the need to go through the IVR since some customers despise them so. For example, using LucyPhone.com, customers can simply enter your company's toll-free number into their iPhone app or the LucyPhone.com website, then LucyPhone does all the calling and waiting instead. Customers don't have to listen to menu prompts or be put on hold to talk to a sales representative or Customer Service Rep. When someone at your company is able to take the customer's call, LucyPhone calls the customer and connects the two of you automatically.

Bottom Line: *Your website connects you to potential customers around the world. Make it easy for them to get in touch and tell you what they want. Don't hide your sales focus; display it for all to see on the homepage.*

The Sales Team
Processing Leads and Interest into Sales

When Jonathan submitted his Quotation Request through the website, it generated an email that was sent to the Sales Team. This is how the process works in such a case:

The USB Superstore uses a distributed team of sales representatives with a sales manager to coordinate them. Each of the sales representatives is trained to have a checklist on-hand that outlines the procedure for processing interest from Leads. In this case, the Auxiliary Support Team includes a graphic designer who will help create the mock-ups of the product with the prospect's logo on it. In this case, that is an image of the product style Jonathan selects with the TechCo logo on it, as well as the price based on quantity and memory size.

Before the sales representative responds to Jonathan, he does two things:

1. He references the Price Schedule to know the production cost of the style that the prospect is interested in purchasing.

2. He sends a message to the members of the Auxiliary Support Team requesting the customized mock-up, which can include a logo pulled from the prospect's website.

The Price Schedule is a collection of dynamic documents stored online, one for each manufacturer that the USB Superstore works with. Using Google Docs, it's easy to set up a configuration where manufacturers can update pricing for the products they offer, and any changes are visible in real time to members of the Sales Team. A Sourcing Agent can coordinate this for you, or you can simply set it up yourself and invite manufacturers into the dynamic document and give instructions on what to do.

These two steps allow the sales representative to create a customer-specific quote, where the price includes a profit margin based on the actual production costs incurred in producing the customer's order. Since members of the Sales Team are commission-based, the sales representatives have an incentive to really understand the prospective customer's needs and provide customer service that warrants a solid markup over the actual production costs. Since the prospect can't access your manufacturers directly, the customer experience becomes the differentiator in the marketplace, determining your place in the value chain for your customers and prospective customers.

> **Calculate sales commissions based on the gross margin created for the company.**
>
> **That way incentives are aligned between the sales team and business owners**

Before we move on, a quick note about the Auxiliary Support Team. In the case of the graphic designer, the USB Superstore set up a service-level agreement (SLA) that requires the designer to create a customized mock-up of the product with the logo within sixty minutes of receiving the request during normal business hours. Since every member of the Auxiliary Support Team is only paid for the amount of quotes produced, there's practically no downside to this arrangement and it allows the sales representative to focus on selling, instead of getting bogged down in administrative details pertaining to each order.

Now that all the information is in place, the sales representative calls the number Jonathan provided and answers any additional questions he may have, such as the projected production time and the shipping charges. Once the graphic designer has the mock-up and custom quote ready, it is sent to the sales representative for review. He adds a profit margin onto the production cost and sends the final mock-up and quote to the client for final review.

As we saw, Jonathan was thrilled with the prompt response time. He had a lot on his plate and getting this issue resolved was one less thing he had to think about. So the company already had the inside track on the sale because Jonathan was going to make a good case for the order with his boss. Having a customized price quote that showed exactly how the drives would look with the TechCo logo went a long way towards successfully making that case. Everyone wins.

> *Bottom Line: Making sales is a function of proposing value to your potential customers. Make yourself and your sales team indispensable by making it easy for your clients to say "Yes!"*
>
> *Create customized price quotes, proactively follow-up and forward information pertinent to their business and don't take it personally if the sale doesn't close. There is always next time.*

Closing The Sale
Creating the Sales Order & Customer Invoice

Once Jonathan has approval to make the purchase, he calls back the sales representative and gives the payment information over the phone. At that point the sales representative creates the Sales Order titled TechCo-101 in the customer relationship management system (CRM), entering all the details that the Production team needs to produce the order, such as the quantity, style, graphics to be used on the drives, etc. He marks the order "paid" and creates the invoice, which is then emailed back to Jonathan along with a request for the graphics files that are needed for production.

Once these files are received, the sales representative uploads them into the TechCo-101 Sales Order and changes the order status to "ready for production". Now the sales representative notifies the Production Team that Sales Order TechCo-101 is ready for actual production. Everything is done via email and the records are updated in real time through the CRM system, which can be accessed via any web browser.

The Production Process
Sourcing Agents and Manufacturers

Finally, we get to the stage where actual production begins. The Production Team has received the Sales Order and it's time to fulfill the order for TechCo. The Production Team consists of a Sourcing Agent who serves as the liaison to the Manufacturers that are used by the USB Superstore. The Sourcing Agent has the leeway to choose the best factory to produce the order for TechCo. He or she also coordinates getting the graphics to them as well as any other information that's needed to produce and fulfill the order.

Since the factories themselves don't have access to the CRM system, the Sourcing Agent conveys the information to the factory on USB Superstore's behalf, such as the delivery address of the order, special packaging requirements, etc. Thus the Sourcing Agent acts as a filter between the business operators and the manufacturers and fulfillment aspects of the business.

SUMMARY OF THE OPERATIONS MODEL
As It Applies to the USB Superstore

So far we have walked through a narrative description of a typical customer sales cycle: how Jonathan found USBsuperstore.com, how he made the purchase and how the order was fulfilled and received. Then we took a more detailed look under the hood, seeing all the processes that occur behind the scenes, out of sight of the customer.

At this point I want you to understand that anything can be sold this way, any physical product you can imagine can be sold using this same process. It is beautiful in its simplicity and its potential. While we've just used a flash drive as an example, you could be selling iPad covers, hand-carved wooden picture frames, children's toys — virtually anything. The Model is the most efficient system for selling products online that find their ways to customers all over the world.

Every sale follows the same process and you can have any number of them going on all at the same time. Because the process is fixed, everything happens in an orderly, predictable matter, so it is entirely scalable – The Model grows right along with you as you make more sales, generate more revenue and increase your market share and customer base. You can also use The Model to create entirely new lines of business.

__Bottom Line:__ The Operations Model provides a business architecture that you can use to offer products and/or services to anyone in the world who also has an Internet connection.

Now let's take a look at each of the components of the Operations Model in detail and focus on how you can design a business that suits your personality...

PAID COST-PER-CLICK TRAFFIC
Instant Traffic to Your Website

Paid Traffic
Google AdWords
(PPC)

One of the greatest advantages of the Internet from the standpoint of a business is that you can draw customers to your website immediately using cost-per-click advertising (CPC). This is particularly important since search engines can take months to fully index your website and display it prominently in the organic search results. That means you can be generating traffic within a day or so of signing up for CPC while others are still waiting for their sites to appear in the search engines naturally.

CPC does cost money. That's because you're paying every time someone clicks on a listing that uses your keywords. Google AdWords (adwords.google.com) is the market leader in this, and in my opinion, the only one you really need to use.

Google not only leads the world of CPC, commanding over 85% market share in Singapore, but they invented the concept of search engine advertising. When you factor in ease of payment and the robust set of tools they have to optimize and track your campaigns, there's really no better value for your advertising dollar.

Your focus in AdWords is to create a campaign that brings the maximum amount of qualified traffic to your site from the largest number of search terms that your customers are likely to use to locate products you sell. Once you've identified the search terms, you want to minimize the cost of each click while increasing the percentage of leads or sales generated through them. This is called "increasing your conversion rate."

Here's How It Works:
For the vast majority of businesses, there is a handful of general terms that can be used to describe the products that are offered. For our purposes, we will refer to these as "Apex Keywords." There are also variations and expansions on these Apex Keywords, which are the actual search terms people will use to search online. We'll call these "Variations."

When someone searches for one of these terms, among either the Apex Keywords or the Variations, small advertisements appear on the right side of the search results screen. The search words determine which ads appear. These are generated through Google AdWords and explain your product or service in three short lines of text.

Google AdWords is a lot like chess. You can learn the basics in just a few hours but it will take a lifetime to master it. There are a lot of companies out there that do nothing else but create, manage and execute AdWords campaigns. While you may want someone else to take charge of this aspect of your business at some point down the road, you really should understand the principles that underpin a successful campaign.

Examples of Apex Keywords, Variations and Ads

Apex Keywords	Keyword Variations	Displayed Advertisement
Wholesale USB	Wholesale USB Flash Drive	Buy Wholesale USB Drives
	Custom Wholesale USB	#1 Rated for Customer Service
	Wholesale USB Provider	Min Order 50 – Free Graphics!
	Wholesale Promo USBs	www.USBsuperstore.com
Bulk Flash	Bulk Flash Drives	Buy Bulk USB Flash Drives
	Buy Bulk Flash Drives	#1 Rated for Customer Service
	Custom Bulk Flash Drives	Min Order 50 – Free Graphics!
	Bulk Promo Flash Drives	www.USBsuperstore.com

Quality Scores And How To Make The Most Of Your Budget

For each campaign, AdWords assigns a Quality Score. This takes into consideration the consistency and relevancy of your keywords and advertisements relative to the actual content on your website. It checks this against the website that is linked to the last line of your ad. The higher your score, the less you pay per click.

The trick is to segment your campaign into separate Ad Groups for each of your Apex Keywords. Then, you want to have the search terms that will display your ad (Variations) contain the Apex Keyword.

Look at the first example above. The Apex Keyword is "Wholesale USB" which is then used in four different Variations. In the ad, it is used as the headline "Buy Wholesale USB Drives". When combined with your website which uses your Apex Keywords in the copy, the hidden tags, and in SEO strategies, you will get the highest quality traffic for the lowest cost-per-click.

Start now at: http://adwords.google.com

How to Secure a High Quality Score

User Activity Flow	**Commentary**
	User searches for "Wholesale USB Drives" which contains the Apex Keyword "Wholesale USB" that is in an Ad Group with the same name...
User Searches for: **Wholesale USB Drives**	
Buy Wholesale USB Drives #1 Rated for Customer Service Min Order 50 - Free Graphics! www.USBsuperstore.com	...so this advertisement is displayed on the right-hand side of the search results page. The headline contains "Wholesale USB"
www.USBsuperstore.com **Metatags:** Wholesale USB, Custom Flash Drives, etc. **Description:** Your resource for wholesale USB flash products, custom USB flash drives, etc. **Site Content:** Welcome to USB Superstore, we hope you enjoy browsing our selection of Wholesale USB products, custom promotional flash drives and accessories... **Menu links:** Wholesale USB Products Custom Flash Drive Solutions About Us, etc.	The domain name contains "USB" and the information visible to search engines indicate that this site is relevant for the term "Wholesale USB" The visible site content emphasizes Wholesale USB among other relevant terms. The menu links reinforce that this site focuses on "Wholesale USB" drives among other things.

Net Effect: Emphasizing Apex Keywords in ads, meta content and visible site content increases your site's Quality Score, which drives down cost-per-click and increases positioning in the search engine results pages.

NON-PAID TRAFFIC (SEO)
Search Engine Optimization

Non-Paid Traffic
Organic Search
(SEO)

While CPC advertising will drive immediate traffic to your website, you can't increase your traffic exponentially with CPC alone. Every click through from your ad costs you money, whether the person who clicked on it ends up buying from you or not. It's a good short-term solution, but in the long term, you want to have a daily stream of traffic to your site that costs you nothing.

You can do this by optimizing your website so that it appears in the main section of the search engine results page (SERP), the organic search results that are based on the content of your site.

You increase your sites' rankings in SERP by proving to the search engines that your website is relevant with respect to the search terms that people use when looking for your products or services. This process is called search engine optimization, or SEO for short.

There are two sides to the SEO equation: On-Site and Off-Site

On-Site SEO: Refers to the naming conventions you use for your URLs, images, title tags and the meta tags, which are in the coding and aren't visible on the pages you see with your browser. This includes the published site description information. If you look at the source code, you'll see all these tags near the top of the page, often with <meta name=> before them. For example, on the usbsuperstore.com site, the invisible tags look like this:

<meta name="keywords" content="wholesale USB, USB products, promotional USB product, promotional USB, printed USB, personalized USB, custom USB, custom flash drive, bulk flash memory, branded USB">

In this example, you can see that the "keywords" meta tag has a bunch of search words in it while the "description" tag is a sentence. As noted, these don't appear on the web page you see. They are purely for the search engines to use and to assist them in ranking your site.

Off-Site SEO: describes the links into your website from other sites. The more heavily trafficked the website is that is linking to you, the more weight your site is given in return. For Google this handicapping system is called PageRank, which is a logarithmic ranking from 1-10 for your site's overall importance on the Internet. For example, if Oprah links to your site, it gets a much higher ranking than a more generic website.

Here's a more detailed look at the factors that affect your rankings:

On-Site SEO	Off-Site SEO
Meta Tags set as Apex Keywords	Links in from knowledge databases
Site Description is self-explanatory	Links from other similar sites
Images Alt Tags set as Apex Keywords	Submitting site to directories
Header Tags are set (not left blank)	Links embedded in anchor tags
Site content emphasizes Apex Keywords	Site indexed by search engines
Sub-URLs are named appropriately	Press releases link to your site
Include a sitemap on your website	Links from highly trafficked sites

COMBINING CPC AND SEO: MAXIMIZING TRAFFIC AND MINIMIZING COST

Google flatly rejects claims that paid advertisers, such as participants in the AdWords program, will get preferential placement in the organic search results. This would undermine the authenticity and objectivity of the search results displayed. It's important to remember that there is no direct correlation between ad dollars spent and Quality Score achieved.

However one of the determinants of your Quality Score is the amount of traffic to your site, and its consistency. This is where AdWords and CPC advertising can help, since it jumpstarts traffic by running AdWords ads on the right-hand side of the search engine results page, which, over time, becomes a factor in determining your Quality Score, assuming you have simultaneously executed an SEO strategy.

You want to use a multifaceted approach to getting a high Quality Score so that it cements your standings in the search engines.

Structuring your website like this optimizes your SEO & PPC efforts:

1. Configuring your website so that you have on-site SEO that is based on your Apex Keywords.
2. Configure your AdWords campaigns to target these Apex Keywords.
3. Make your website active and fund your AdWords campaign. Traffic will begin to flow to your site through the campaign.

4. Work your Off-Site SEO strategies (such as getting links to your website) to reinforce all your On-Site SEO.

THE
GO LIVE
STRATEGY

Your Ideal Launch Scenario Should Look Like This:

Launch your website with on-site SEO in place and then fund your AdWords campaign for the first time.

At the same time you start the off-site SEO campaign, begin a publishing schedule for content on your site's blog. Search engines love blogs and rank their content higher based on the frequency at which new content is published.

Submit some articles to knowledge databases with links to your site embedded in anchor tags that are specific to your Apex Keywords. Initially, all of your traffic is from CPC. But as your site begins to gain traction, your traffic will begin to be a mix of CPC and SEO-based traffic. You monitor all of this from the Google Analytics account which tracks all activity on your site.

The Goal: Be on the first page of the organic search results for numerous terms relevant to your business, and have CPC as an available option, not a necessity, for driving additional traffic.

In other words, you want to receive as much traffic as you can from your SEO strategies because SEO means free traffic and free leads, as opposed to CPC, which has a cost per lead.

And now I'd like to introduce a friend and colleague, Gael Breton, who knows more about SEO than 99% of the people on earth. He is the Managing Director of Higher Click, an SEO provider from Hungary that I've worked with on many projects.

I am pleased that Gael agreed to write a guest featurette for this book with some great SEO strategies. With no further ado, I turn the floor over to Gael...

SEO FOR LIFESTYLE ENTREPRENEURS

By: Gael Breton of HigherClick.com

So you've taken the first steps towards becoming a Lifestyle Entrepreneur? Great idea! Search engine marketing is probably the most effective ways to promote a newly created business or product these days. In a matter of hours, you can reach hundreds of thousands of potential customers if what you produce goes viral like the Bucky balls recently (http://www.getbuckyballs.com/) featured by Google on their home page for one day, the owner of the site recorded over $100,000 in sales in 24 hours.

However, success stories like these are not the daily bread and butter for most online product-oriented business owners. The Internet was a new frontier for business 10 years ago, ripe with opportunity and without much sophisticated competition. Nowadays however, the absence of a well-planned strategy greatly reduces your odds for success as more and more businesses migrate from physical retail to digital storefronts.

Here are some steps you should consider while working on your SEO and getting highly-qualified traffic (i.e.: prospective customers!) from the search engines.

1 — Match the offer and demand

When you talk to most business people, they will generally commonly agree with the fact that launching yourself on the market without prior market study greatly reduces the odds of success. Well, same goes with the online world and especially SEO. Prior to even designing your website you should already think about search and how people are going to find your online business through the search engines.

Today, the best way to find out about who searches for what on search engines is to use the data search engines themselves let users access through their paid advertising programs, AdWords for Google and AdCenter for Bing and Yahoo.

I strongly advise you to use these tools to match your content with what people are looking for; there is no point for you to tailor your efforts towards something that has no audience on the web, even if it seems like the best solution at the time.

In order to use this helpful tool, simply type in the keywords you think best represent your business and select your physical target market (geo-location and language) and Google will suggest the most popular keywords searches related to the keyword(s) you just typed. My advice is to select 3 to 4 terms per converting page of your website, going for more will simply dilute the effort. By "converting page" I mean the actual URL of you website where people are encouraged to buy your products.

Here is the URL of Google keyword tool:
https://adwords.google.com/select/KeywordToolExternal

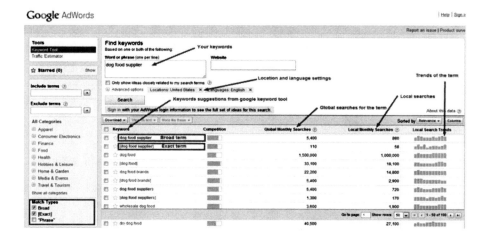

2 — Optimize your website

Once you are done with selecting keywords that both match your content and have significant traffic, it is now time to tell search engines that your website is all about these keywords and also make sure the website is easily accessible for them.

Back in the days, the number of times your keyword occurred on your page was the most important thing. These days, with modern search engines, the rules are slightly different. What really matters is to have your keywords on the right spots. Here is a little checklist that will help you optimize your pages:

- Put your keywords in the title tag
- Bold your keywords on your page
- Put your keywords in your headers
- Make sure you have a sitemap.xml and you have submitted it to Google webmasters tools (http://www.google.com/webmasters/tools/)
- Deny search engines access to your admin areas through your robots.txt
- Optimize your page loading speed by combining all your css and javascript files
- Reduce the number of outgoing links on your pages

Once you have done all that, your website should be fairly well optimized in order to ensure optimal search engine rankings.

3 — Get the world to know about your website

Now that you know what keywords you want to rank for and have optimized your pages, it is now time to let the world (and the search engines) know about your website.

The objective here is going to try and get a maximum of links back to your website and if possible, have those links point to your website with the keywords you want to rank for as anchor text.

There are plenty of ways to acquire links, some of them easier than others, however, keep in mind that the hardest links to get are also the most valuable ones in the eyes of the search engines most of the time.

Here are a few tips for you to earn quality links for your newly built website:

A — Guest Blogging

This is a very easy technique you can apply to pretty much any niche. All you have to do is to find bloggers blogging about topics related to your topic and offer them to write a blog post for them in exchange for a link back to your site. This will help you both reach out to an audience interested in what you are doing and getting a high quality link for search engines.

B — Niche Directory Submission

These days, directory submissions are generally considered as low quality link building. However, if you do a bit of research and find directories specialized in your niche, this is a different story. Google places a lot of weight on relevancy. If a link to your site is placed on a website with topical correlation to yours, then it does have a lot of extra weight. Usually, it just takes a Google search to find these directories and then submit your website in there.

C — Social Media Marketing

Often considered as low quality links, social media links have long been excluded from most SEO strategies. However, as the Internet evolved to revolve more and more around the sociosphere, so have search engine's algorithms. As Matt Cutts, head of the spam section in Google suggests in this video (http://www.youtube.com/user/GoogleWebmasterHelp#p/u/12/ofhwPC-5Ub4) what this suggests is not to spam your links on your Facebook wall but rather to find authorities on social medias to tweet about your website and share it on their Facebook pages, this does also help attracting traffic and make your website viral.

Hopefully this overview and a few select tips will help you on your way to building a sustainably profitable Lifestyle Entrepreneurship business! As a longtime partner and fan of Jesse Krieger we look forward to working with you sometime soon to help realize your Vision through the exciting world of online entrepreneurship.

Best of luck,

Gael Breton
Managing Director of HigherClick.com

REFERRAL TRAFFIC
Social Media & CPA Marketing

Social Media
Activity-Based
(CPA)

Of course, there are a lot of other ways to generate traffic to your site beyond CPC and SEO, which focus entirely on drawing traffic from search engines. While it is certainly possible to build a great business from search engine marketing (SEO + PPC), there is no real marginal cost to employing a social media strategy.

In fact, once you've created your logo, branding and general company look and feel, the hard work is done; social media is just an extension of the brand image into new arenas where new customers can be found and communicated with.

Let's focus on Facebook since it is now one of the most heavily trafficked websites on the Internet. The site continues to grow and innovate, and is maturing as a viable marketing outlet for businesses. Underneath the "Sign In" button on Facebook.com you can create a business page. Enter the basic info and that's it!

Once you have set up your business page on Facebook, anyone can click on the Like button and your page will be instantly linked to their profile.

Select the type of page you want to create, assign it a name, click that you are the designated representative, then click on "Create Official Page" and you're in business. From there, you can customize it to fit your needs, adding your logo, photos, product or service information, links, etc.

The next step is to attract people to your site. You can do this by using the Facebook Ads feature and inviting all your friends and associates who have their own pages on Facebook to "Like" you.

One of the great advantages of Facebook is that you can communicate and interact with your customers without necessarily letting them connect to your actual circle of friends. You can also try the various social plug-ins Facebook offers so you can add a Facebook Share button on your website. Then add your Facebook page to your standard email signature and cross-link it to your other marketing initiatives and campaigns.

Once you have your Facebook page set up and have an audience, market to them. Try to set a periodic publishing schedule and continue to deliver some small form of value to your audience on an ongoing basis. To build a loyal following on Facebook, and actually make some money doing so, you can experiment with "Facebook Only" promotions, offering a discount or special pricing to people who visit your site from Facebook in a specified period of time.

Your social media content *can be anything from new product announcements to helpful tips and tricks about your offerings. Like any other interactive marketing strategy, you want to* build a sense of community *on the site, encouraging visitors to* communicate and participate.

> ***Bottom Line:*** *Facebook doesn't cost anything but your time. It's free marketing and offers a potentially huge audience for your products and services, if you're willing to invest the time and effort to set up and execute a social media strategy.*

TWITTER: THE POWER OF 140 CHARACTERS

No doubt you have heard about Twitter by now. The real-time conversation tool where you post messages no longer than 140 characters is fast becoming as popular as Facebook. But the two are not the same. Therefore, your Twitter strategy, should you choose to employ one, should complement your other social media endeavors.

Twitter is great for publishing an eye-grabbing headline and a link to a website with long-form content (i.e. more than 140 characters). Examples of the utility of a tool like this are:

- Reposting blogs and RSS feeds to your Twitter followers
- Publishing time-sensitive deals and special offers
- Responding to customer queries in real time

- Finding new potential customers that are writing about products similar to what you sell

It is super easy to set up a Twitter account and begin posting and building up followers. Just go to www.Twitter.com and sign up. Be sure to create a screen name that directly describes your business. Once you are set up, fill in the pertinent information on your profile and upload either a picture or your logo as your profile picture.

Now you want to start "Following" people that are talking about products and issues that relate to your industry. This is not too difficult either, just enter a couple of search terms or product names that are similar to yours and see who comes up. There is no limit on how many people you follow or how many people follow you, so don't be too selective. Often, if you follow people they will, in turn, follow you as well.

Once you're set up and have an initial group of people that you are following, it is time to integrate your Twitter account to a service that lets you leverage your Twitter account for business purposes. That means publishing regularly and integrating some of these utilities into your Twitter strategy:

TOP 5 TWITTER UTILITIES YOU SHOULD KNOW

1. **Bit.ly** - This is a link-shortner that allows you to consolidate links into about 20 characters and also provides analytics so you can see how many people click your link and/or "retweet" your message.

2. **Twitpic.com** - The easiest way to integrate photos into your Twitter stream. You send the picture to a custom email address and include your message in the subject line.

3. **Tweetscan.com** - This lets you scan Twitter for topics of interest and receive updates on who's talking about what. Similar to Google Alerts and a great way to track brands on Twitter.

4. **Hootsuite.com** - Nice business application that lets you queue up tweets that will be published according to a schedule you define. Also has a bunch of tools to track viewership, engagement and even translates tweets into other languages!

5. **Twuffer.com** - Something akin to Hootsuite lite. Easy scheduler to line up a bunch of tweets in advance and have them automatically posted to your page.

Social media marketing has a noted emphasis on developments in real-time, exclusivity and privileges afforded to those in your community of interest.

> **Bottom Line:** *If you can provide frequent, timely updates and news over time, then you will begin to build a stickiness with your customers and followers that breeds loyalty. Since you have an online Lifestyle Entrepreneurship business, the community-building and customer relations aspects of your business will take place online (surprise!).Putting Theory Into Practice*

Vision-MAP for Social Media Marketing

Here is a sample Vision-MAP for a good Social Media marketing strategy. Feel free to use this as-is, or modify it to fit your own business and personal objectives and value system.

- **VISION**: Build a community of interest around my brand, products and solutions through social media marketing.

- **MISSION**: Add value to the community through exclusive offers and expedited response to customer queries. Respect and learn from customer experiences, especially if they are negative.

- **ACTIONS**: Create and maintain a posting schedule. Announce maximum response time to customer questions. Induce sales and re-orders through personal attention to customers. Cite and repost valuable information from other companies and contributors in your industry. Grow the community by interacting with both customers and other businesses.

- **PRODUCT**: Track referral traffic from Facebook and Twitter via Analytics. Compare conversions between social media channel and SEO/PPC channel. Publish polls on Facebook and Twitter to gauge customer experiences. Ensure that "exclusive offers" still remain profitable, or at least that they are loss-leaders to future profitable customer interactions.

ANALYTICS: THE ART OF TRAFFIC ANALYSIS

Understanding where your visitors comes from, how they interact, and what path they take towards purchasing from you is crucial. Thankfully, Google Analytics lets you access an amazing amount of data about your site and your customers. Every aspect of your visitors' activity can be tracked, including the time of day they visit most, the country of origin, the web browser they used, the pages they visited the most and how long they stayed there.

Best of all, it's free!

Once you understand how users interact with your site, you can make informed decisions about what products to feature where, and how to lay out the site to make it a more intuitive experience for the visitor. Here are some of the key metrics to focus on when using Google Analytics:

Bounce Rate: This metric shows the percent of people who click into your home page and then hit the back button on their browser. It shows how relevant or compelling your homepage was with respect to what the visitor was searching for and expecting.

If you just launched and are using AdWords only (as you work on your SEO, of course), a bounce rate of 50% isn't bad, although ideally, you want it to be much lower. Remember though, you can have a 30% bounce rate with a fully executed SEO and CPC campaign strategy and still make a good profit. To lower your bounce rate, experiment with A/B testing for the home page to see what content visitors respond to best.

Time on Site & Page Views: This is a measure of engagement for your site. If your main call to action is to submit a quotation request from the home page, then one to two minutes spent on the site and an average of one to two page views isn't bad. But if you want your visitor to look through your catalog and review other pages of important content, and you have these numbers, then you should simplify your site, simplify your message and have only one or two primary calls to action.

Geo-Location of Visitors: This is a great tool if you're targeting certain geographic locations. It also gives you some insight into how you're ranking on foreign search engines if you notice a lot of international traffic. Let's say you're selling bed spreads and quilts.

There's no point in eating up your ad budget marketing to Malaysians and Singaporeans who are sweltering in the summer heat. Better to change your on-site SEO and Apex Keywords to focus more on the areas where your target audience is actually cold and would consider a purchase. AdWords allows you to do geo-targeting, so you can focus on certain parts of the country if you wish, instead of the entire country. This is terrific for niche products.

Goals & Conversion Rates: This allows you to define a goal for your site, such as submitting a quote request, getting an order placed or getting a sign up for your newsletter. Then you track which search term visitors are using to find your site and completing your goal. Once you get a large enough sample size from this metric, you will see what search terms (i.e. the Variations of Apex Keywords) are converting into Goals.

The bottom line: Analyzing and understanding traffic trends and stats is essential to your success. While getting a lot of traffic is good for the ego, you want to focus on conversions. If only fifty people visit your site in a month and twenty-five of them complete a Goal, that's fantastic! Your conversion rate is 50%. Do further experimentation with your search term Variations to see if you can increase it even more.

Start now at: google.com.analytics

SELLING THE DREAM:
CLOSING THE SALE & FUNDING YOUR LIFESTYLE

Closing sales is the growth engine for your business. How well your sales team can convert leads into sales defines the horsepower for your business' engine. In other words, your sales team's ability is one of the primary determinants of how quickly you can grow and scale your business.

Within The Operations Model, this is the most important function. For our purposes, we want the customer to indicate their interest through a quote request or a phone call. If you've set up your SEO and advertising right you'll be focusing on qualifying prospective customer's interests, which is much more enjoyable to outbound "cold call" type of sales. Ideally, the customer has already done some of the sales process for you by searching for products in your industry, and liking your website enough to contact you.

This type of selling is far more enjoyable since you're really not selling in the traditional sense. Rather, you're responding to a prospect's actual interest in your products or services. In the process, you get to meet people from all walks of life who want to become your customers. You will learn a tremendous amount about what buyers in your industry are looking for, and get new ideas for product configurations and special offers you can provide. Always try to be responsive to what your prospective customers actually want (as opposed to what you *think* they want).

There are some basics in selling that hold true across the board regardless of what industry you're in; then there are other aspects that are industry-specific, and which differentiate you from the competition.

To be successful you need to have a grasp on the basics of selling and, over time, attain an advanced understanding of the differentiators in your industry.

There's no shortage of talented, experienced sales people out there. For them to be of maximum benefit to your business, you need to equip them with the industry-specific knowledge and competitive differentiators that will help them close the most sales, as well as align their incentives so they augment your business' bottom line.

Here is a quick exercise to determine industry-specific knowledge:

1. Do some searches for different keywords that describe products in your industry.
2. Contact every company that appears on the first page of the search results (the advertisers as well as the organic search results).
3. Be very aware of how they interact with you. What could they do better? What would you do if you were selling their product?
4. Take notes on what they emphasize or recommend to you.
5. Ask for additional information and see how long it takes them to respond.
6. When they do respond, note if it was an impersonal, templated response or a personalized letter.

THE SKILLS THAT PAY THE BILLS
What Your Sales Team Needs to Succeed

Fundamental Sales Skills:
Ability to quickly build rapport with potential customers. Whenever you or your sales team is on a call with a prospect, remember to smile, be upbeat and optimistic and genuinely enthusiastic to be talking about your products.

Quick response time after the lead is initially submitted. Set up a rule based on how realistic it is in your industry that you will respond to quote requests or sales inquiries within a certain time. Make this a selling point on the website and live up to it. If your marketing says "Submit a quote request and receive a call back within 1 hour" then you need to make sure that happens every time.

Proactively make suggestions to learn what the customer needs. Of course the call is focused on the sale, but that doesn't mean you can't be friendly and offer suggestions to see what specifically it is the customer wants. If you are proactive and make recommendations, the customer may see things in a way they had not before.

Determine budgets and decision-making authority early. Nothing is more frustrating than talking for 15 or 20 minutes just to find out the prospect doesn't have authority to make a purchase and needs to "talk to his boss" and call you back. Try to find out early on whether the person you're talking to is doing research for his boss, or is actually a decision maker who can buy from you.

Define value propositions clearly and add value with each contact. Whatever your key value propositions are, make sure you communicate them to the customer in no uncertain terms. If you have multiple sales calls before a close, make sure to bring something new to the table each time. This doesn't need to be discounting or offering freebies, but can be as simple as sharing news pertinent to their industry or offering to put them in touch with someone that may be interested in buying their products. These small gestures add up and set you apart from others who just want to close the sale as fast as possible.

Offer incentives to close the sale quickly and get paid up front. If a customer is just about ready to buy but wants to think about just a little longer, that is the time to offer a discount or a sweetener if they close the deal right away. This could be something like a 2% discount and free shipping or extra warranty coverage. Something that isn't too expensive to you (the company) but still incentivizes them to buy now instead of later. I think it was Confucius who said "a bird in the hand is worth two in the bush." Getting 98% of the sales price right away is better than 0% later.

Follow the ABCs: Always Be Closing. Each time you talk to a potential customer make sure you are moving towards closing the sale. Don't entertain aimless conversations or disclose information about how your business operates. If you think the prospect may be working for a competitor or just fishing for information, politely tell them to get back in touch when they are ready to make a purchase then move on.

Industry-Specific Knowledge and Positioning

What differentiates your product from your competitors? Your potential customers are most likely looking at other providers in your industry around the same time they are contacting you. You need to be able to describe what specifically sets you apart from the other companies.

Can you offer something for free that others charge for? Even though we like to think of ourselves as rational decision makers and good negotiators, it is hard to disregard the appeal of something for "free". Even if it is fairly clear that the cost is being bundled into the overall price or (even better) incurs no cost to you to give away, it still sounds good to include "free shipping" or "free graphics with orders of 100 units or more".

Can you provide a simplified pricing structure relative to others? Some companies have the most confusing pricing structures, or are just totally unclear about how much their services will cost in total. Don't be that company. Spend a little extra time to create a simplified price structure that makes it intuitive for a customer to understand the value. To visualize this watch some late-night infomercials where they describe all the things you'll get in extensive detail "all for the one-time only price of $19.95".

Is your product of a higher quality than that of others? If your main differentiator is a much higher quality product than others on the market, make that your main selling point. When talking to customers, describe situations where people went for the lower cost option only to have a cheap product that broke a week or two after they bought it. Focus on how reliability and durability set your product apart. However, if you are selling products that are generally available or commoditized emphasize the customer service or satisfaction guarantee.

FINDING YOUR SALES STRATEGY

"Cross The River By Feeling The Stones"

— Deng Xiaoping

Taking into account the tips above regarding general sales skills and industry-specific knowledge, you will ultimately develop your own unique sales strategy. In doing so, Deng Xiaoping's advice proves helpful; to cross the river "by feeling the stones" basically means that you should move slowly and feel out each step before you move to the next one. Start by offering what you think is a reasonable product at a fair price, and try out different tactics to improve effectiveness. But don't change your whole approach if something is not working, move carefully and identify just what it is that will set you apart from the pack.

> Adapt your sales approach one step at a time. Start from a firm footing, and try different offers and incentives one-by-one until you have the most compelling sales story in your industry.

Keep in mind that some, if not many, of the industry-specific positioning points you'll be able to deliver on will depend on your relationships with suppliers and partner firms in your industry. For example, when I was running USB Superstore, our manufacturers offered a 12-month warranty on all flash drives sold. We re-packaged that as our own 12-month guarantee and offered it to each of our customers.

The value of offering an extended warranty like this is helpful when making the sale as it provides customers with a sense of security. The reality is less than a handful of customers ever took advantage of the warranty, despite an industry-wide 1-2% failure rate on flash drives. When one or two flash drives out of an order of 250 failed, it usually wasn't worth the customer's time to pursue replacing them. The net result was that we were covered on the back-end (the factory would replace them for free) and it provided additional sales ammunition on the front end. Those are the kind of win-wins that you need to identify in your industry, specific to your offer.

LIFESTYLE ENTREPRENEUR IN-FOCUS: ANDREW YEOH
Co-Founder of Sports Food (www.sportsfoodco.com)

Over the last year or two, Andrew and I have hung out, coached clients and partied like rockstars in Miami, Las Vegas, San Francisco, Stockholm, Montreal and even Koh Phangan, Thailand (yup, same Andrew from the Prologue!) He is someone I've always admired for constantly raising the bar. Whether its health and fitness, lifestyle design or entrepreneurship, Andrew always strives for superlative achievement and, although there are always ups and downs on the road to success, Andrew always appears to be breaching new heights of excellence. So it's no surprise that when I asked him to answer a few questions so I could write a feature about him for Lifestyle Entrepreneur, he basically did my job for me! With no further ado, I'm turning over the typewriter to Andrew Yeoh, co-founder of Sports Food and a core instructor on Project Rockstar:

Jesse: What were your circumstances growing up? How did your upbringing influence your desire to live the life you have now?

Andrew: I grew up in a very suburban neighborhood an hour outside of San Francisco and am a first generation American. They'll never admit to it but my parents gave up the comforts of friends, family and everything they knew to move to America. Them doing what they did so I could access the world of opportunity I've been presented with is something that's always resonated with me. To this day they've never once asked for recognition. That level of unconditional sacrifice and love is something that's sparked a desire in myself to reach high and refuse a life where I feel like I'm settling, especially if it's out of fear or comfort. Moreover, it's instilled a desire to build a life defined by freedom and flexibility, things my parents were probably seeking when they moved to the US. As I've gotten older, that desire has continued to build. Now I can hardly imagine a life that wasn't fully on my own terms. I think that's a good thing.

Q: What was your first experience in business, how did it end up, and what were the learning lessons you took away from it?

While I was still working in the corporate world as an investment banker my first foray into business was an attempted acquisition of an existing small business.

Deep down I knew I wanted to properly start my own thing but I still held the limiting belief that I just didn't possess the creativity to do so. It seemed like buying something existing was the only realistic shot I had. Ultimately the deal fell through, then the next three potential deals also fell through. I felt hopeless and crushed. A lot of lessons came through this though.

Through meeting all these different business owners I realized entrepreneurship did not necessarily equate to freedom. If I wanted freedom it had to be a very particular type of business with the right infrastructure, ability to scale through the internet, and a virtually manageable workflow. From a leadership standpoint I also saw the importance of picking the right people to partner with, as it seemed to be the case that failing partnerships were often the cause for many of the failing businesses I was coming across. Lastly, I learned the most important lesson – that if everything was to be exactly the way I wanted it, starting something from scratch was almost unavoidable. These lessons would eventually pave the road and lay the foundation for Sports Food.

Q: Did you have mentors, advisors or inspirational people in your life that drove you towards entrepreneurship? What was their best advice to you?

Two extremely successful business mentors immediately come to mind, Jim and Andy. Jim is the youngest multi-millionaire I know and his path to success is littered with many life lessons. He has a rock solid work ethic, is fearless of failure, and is always intensely pushing boundaries. The best advice I've ever received from Jim was the idea that if I tried something entrepreneurial and it failed, I would find something else, and if that failed, I would keep finding a "something else" until something finally hit. That really helped build the confidence and trust within myself to take a leap of faith into becoming an entrepreneur.

> It dawned on me that at a core level my freedom and the desire to fully be my own man was something I not just wanted, but needed.

When I first met Andy I was really impressed by the life he was leading. He had already built a successful business that provided him the freedom to do whatever he wanted whenever he wanted. He traveled frequently, had depth of character, and was good with people. The biggest lesson I learned from him was that others will often try to keep you on the beaten path when you're working to break free. But that it's in those moments when everyone seems to doubt you that you have to beat to your own drum and fight your own fight. Having come from a traditional corporate job, this was a huge shift in perception – to realize that sometimes it was best to just tune everyone else out.

Come to think of it, if it weren't for the impact of mentors I probably would still be working a desk job. I sure as hell wouldn't be

> **The company was structured with the core concept of being able to "be where we wanted to be, when we wanted to be there."**

anywhere near where I am now, and Sports Food would probably still be struggling in its infancy. Mentors really are the shortcut to life, you can achieve years of hard-earned experience in the span of a conversation and save yourself a ton of time and frustration. Finding one is not just all about luck. Mentors generally love people who work hard and take action. If you can display that you're that kind of person, and you're personable and enjoyable to be around, there's more people willing to help than you may think.

Q: What is your business now and how is it structured so it can be run from anywhere in the world with a laptop and an internet connection?

I am the co-founder of Sports Food (www.sportsfoodco.com), a sports nutrition and lifestyle brand. Sports Food embodies the way sports nutrition should be, a modern face in an aging industry. The sports nutrition space is was filled with clunky websites, confusing product ranges, and difficult or non-existent shopping functionality. When my partners and I entered the market we understood this didn't really fit with the modern day athlete or fitness enthusiast. He probably doesn't have the time or inclination to drive to a brick and motor store to restock his sports nutrition needs, and probably has even less interest in sifting through an aisle of confusingly named products and supplements. So we set out to build a brand with the customer in mind – a range of proven supplements, top tier customer service, and a state of the art website shopping experience.

With a global landscape and the world being more interconnected than ever before, I am able to essentially run Sports Food from anywhere in the world. I rely on technology, social media, and a worldwide partnership to keep Sports Food nimble. The sports nutrition industry is a constantly changing one, so being able to adapt quickly is extremely important. Partnering with the right experts and building long-lasting relationships crafted on the foundation of mutual respect has been key to making this work. Social media managers in Los Angeles, developers in India,

> Just like some people pay monthly rent in one city for years on end, for me, picking a place, living there for 3-5 weeks, then moving onto somewhere else has become a way of life. It seems very normal to me now.

web designers in Indonesia, manufacturing in California, copywriting in Canada, warehousing in Missouri, label printers in Florida, there is always someone keeping the Sports Food motor running at any given time of day. All these elements are tied by a virtual string to my business partners and me. Like captains of a ship we guide the workflows so they mesh seamlessly. We step in further when we need to, usually in the form of contract negotiations, project management, and brand innovation – all things that can be done virtually.

Q: Give an overview for the last year of your life. What new inspiration or ideas did you uncover that you are putting into practice this year?

Spanning 19 countries and over 35 cities, the last year has represented a lifetime of travel in a handful of months. I've probably missed a few but here's the list that immediately comes to mind.

Australia – Cairns, Sydney
Belgium – Brussels
Bulgaria – Sofia
Canada – Montreal, Treaty Island
China – Hong Kong, Macau
Croatia – Dubrovnik, Hvar, Komiza, Split, Vis
Finland – Lapland
Germany – Berlin
Hungary – Budapest
Malaysia – Langkawi, Penang
Mexico – Cabo San Lucas
Norway – Oslo
Poland – Krakow
Sweden – Stockholm, Linkoping
Taiwan – Taipei
Thailand – Bangkok, Kho Phangan
Turkey – Istanbul

United Kingdom – Hull, London

United States – Atlantic City, Chicago, Las Vegas, Miami, New York City, San Francisco

Some of the standout memories include dogsledding in the North Pole, diving with giant turtles off the Great Barrier Reef, island hopping on a yacht for a week in the Mediterranean, playing cards with one of the founders of Home Depot in his palatial mansion, living on a private resort tucked away in a 10 million year old rainforest with a renowned private beach, and leading a life altering summer mentorship program for a group of likeminded entrepreneurs. An encyclopedia of memories I will look back on for many years to come.

I've met so many sources of inspiration along the way, each with unique perspectives to offer. For instance, we saw first hand how one of the fastest growing sports nutrition brands in Australia had exploded their presence through a creative athlete sponsorship program. We're in the works of building our own program at Sports Food and will be rolling it out later this year. In the UK I was exposed to the ways in which the European market has really embraced a modern face of sports nutrition, through online shopping, a demand for extremely high levels of customer service, and a hunger for innovative products. This really helped shaped the direction of Sports Food and has put us ahead of the curve here in our US home market. It's amazing the kind of innovations you can import globally that represent some really smart ways of doing things.

Q: What is your best advice to aspiring Lifestyle Entrepreneurs?

My advice would be to make the commitment, force some trust in yourself, and then start taking action. Waiting for the exact moment in the future when you formulate the perfect plan is a myth, so is the idea of only striking when the iron is hot. Rather, it's the very act of relentlessly striking day and night that builds success. A practical shortcut for all this is to learn how to create new addictions for yourself. The moment I created a personal addiction to Sports Food is when things really started taking off. I changed the background of my laptop to the Sports Food logo, then did the same for my phone. I set the default pages across all my web browsers to the homepages of our biggest competitors. I subscribed to as many of their weekly mailouts as I could too. Soon after, all I could think about was Sports Food and sports nutrition. That's when work stopped feeling like work.

On the surface my life looks amazing. But people will see what they want to see… usually just the constant stream of new travel, unique experiences, and good times. So it's easy to come to the conclusion that it's a very easy life. But if you peel behind the curtain it's one fueled by countless late nights, 14+ hour workdays, a constant battle against self-doubt, and a never-ending cycle of having to overcome inevitable obstacles and failures. There's no way around it: I work painfully hard, and so do my business partners. It's the unavoidable lifeblood entrepreneurship demands and the price you pay for a life most only dream of. So my advice? Take a chance, feel the fear, and act in spite of it. Then work, work, work.

BUILD
YOUR
CASTLE IN
THE HUMAN
CLOUD

Find and Hire Top Talent on www.Elance.com

Not too long ago, it could be fairly difficult to find talented, professional service providers online. The online platforms and clearing houses for talent were not nearly as populated and accessible as they are today. Communication needed to take place offline for some time-sensitive tasks like proofing graphics, or reviewing concepts for website design.

In today's 21st century Internet economy, you can sub-contract nearly every aspect of your business online. From logo design and building an AdWords campaigns, to your legal and accounting functions, www. Elance.com lives up to its tagline as The Human Cloud to connect you with experts to perform all these functions on your behalf.

> In today's 21st century Internet economy, you can sub-contract nearly every aspect of your business online.
>
> Elance provides the platform to do so.

Online platforms are more robust now, and even incorporate escrow services and conflict resolution, which is both an added safety measure and an enormous time saver if there are problems.

There are hundreds of thousands of highly qualified service providers out there who are more than happy to take on your project and deliver a top quality solution for an agreed price.

They may still be just down the street or they could be located half a world away. It doesn't really matter anymore.

The value proposition of www.Elance.com is clear: Hire and manage talented teams and individuals online, securely and at very competitive prices. As a Lifestyle Entrepreneur, I can't think of a better way to build and manage a business that supports (not interferes with) your lifestyle!

A LOOK UNDER THE HOOD OF WWW.ELANCE.COM

You can think of Elance.com as a giant auction house for talent; You post a job description and professionals bid on your project. After reviewing the bids, you select the provider who you think is most qualified to do the job for the price you want to pay.

Setting up a job is easy and free, although you can feature a job listing for $25. After you create an account, you click on the Hire link, select Post A Job and fill out a short description of what you're looking for. This includes a description of the work to be done, how much you want to pay for it, your desired deadline and how you're going to pay for it.

Once you have all the parameters of the job listed to your satisfaction, make the job active. Almost immediately, you'll start getting bids in from vendors.

At this point, I'd like to introduce a trusted Elance provider Robb Z. from CommuniCreations. Robb has been a service provider on Elance for years and specializes in writing copy for websites, blogs and marketing materials. He has graciously agreed to share his perspective on Elance.com and how to get the best deals.

Introducing: Robb Z. of CommuniCreations, take it away...

Hi everyone, and thanks to Jesse for the invite! Although this book is about how you guys can start your own online businesses, I just want to say that it's also fun to work as a provider through Elance.com.

If you like delivering custom solutions to clients online (Type 1 business) being an Elance provider can provide many of the same freedoms allowed by starting your own company, such as being able to work from anywhere. Anyhow, good luck on your journey, and here are some pointers from my years of working on Elance.com:

<u>Don't award the job to the first people that bid.</u> Get most of your bids in. A lot of the seasoned professionals will watch the job and see what others are bidding on it. They may wait a couple of days before submitting their bid. Usually the first people placing a bid and offering the lower cost are the new providers who don't have a track record of success.

When reviewing bids, consider their experience. These sites actually qualify the providers to make sure they really have the skills they say they do. If you look at their profile, you can see how they tested, whether they have any verified credentials and what their feedback is. This is perhaps the most important part of selecting a bidder. You want to see what their other clients thought of their work and whether they encountered any problems during the project.

When you award a job, define the terms and milestones. It's not unusual for a provider to request a deposit for the project and then additional payments as key milestones are reached. Don't be put off by this – it protects them from having a client walk off with their work without paying for it. And it gives you leverage when making payments based on specific milestones.

Use the Escrow function for safety, but don't fund it all up-front. The best way to deal with financing your project is to use the free escrow service provided by Elance, just don't fund the whole project up front. A good practice is to offer an incentive when the you award the project, then fund escrow as the work is being done.

Use Milestones to break a project down into discrete steps. This way you never have more than a couple hundred dollars of expenses at a time. This lets you start down the path of developing an idea with the freedom to cancel it if you lose interest, and without a large expense or sunk cost. Use this bit of assurance to just go ahead and try out any idea you are playing with.

When you post a project, be extremely specific about what you need. This will help you get bids and proposals that are comparable so you can make an informed decision. Also, never use hourly rates in soliciting bids. Decide on the budget you want to spend (often, it's expressed in terms of Under $500, $500 to $1,000, etc.) and make it clear if you want the bid submitted in a specific way. For example, you can add "Not to exceed $200" in the project description, so bidders don't bother you with a bid that is more than you are willing to pay.

You should know that the bids do factor in the fees these sites charge. The fee is somewhere between 7% and 9.5%. This is how Elance makes money. Your listing of the project is free. The provider has to pay a "marketing fee" or "finder's fee" to work on it.

Best of luck,
Robb Z. of CommuniCreations

A big thanks to Robb Z. for giving us a view from the service provider's perspective! I was among the first generation of Elance clients and routinely spend tens of thousands of dollars on Elance hiring teams to build and manage my Lifestyle Entrepreneur businesses. However, I have never worked as a service provider like Robb, so it is interesting to see both sides of the equation.

Now let's look at a few more tips and tricks regarding Elance.com before we zoom out and focus on some best practices for launching and growing your online Lifestyle Entrepreneur business...

WORKING ON YOUR PROJECT ON ELANCE.COM

Once you've selected your provider and agreed to the terms, you can get to work. These sites have built in workrooms you can use to communicate with one another, review work, link to URLs and conduct virtual meetings. It's very easy to use. Once your project is active you will receive emails from elance.com or Guru.com telling you that something has been posted or added to your workroom. You can respond directly through your email to the provider. It's a remarkably sophisticated, robust system that is extremely easy to use.

An Added Benefit For When Things Go Sour

If you have a dispute with your vendor, Elance and Guru will work as the intermediary between the both of you. They will review the communications in the workroom and the job history. This is why it's so important that you communicate and interact directly through the workroom and don't use personal emails. The thread of communications is key to resolving a dispute and getting your money back, if the decision falls in your favor.

Providing Feedback

Once the job is complete, you will be asked to leave feedback. Remember that this is a double-edged sword. While you may want to ding the vendor for an issue, they can post feedback about you on your site as well. The feedback scores are very important marketing tools and even though you might want to give them all zeros, think twice. It may have just been a personality clash between the two of you that has nothing to do with their everyday performance. This is especially true if you're working with a vendor who has a 4.8 to 5.0 rating on their profile. Obviously, they are known for doing top quality work. The two of you may just not have seen eye to eye on this particular project, or maybe they had a personal issue they were dealing with at the time that you're unaware of.

Give the Guy a Break?

One of the great things about these feedback systems is it gives you the chance to decide whether you want to use a top performing vendor with high scores and dozens of happy clients or try out someone who gave you a really great price but is just starting out and either doesn't have feedback, or doesn't have the best feedback.

This is your choice, of course, but in our experience, you get what you pay for and they may not have feedback for a reason. Or they may have come from another similar site (i.e. a Guru.com freelancer didn't do well there and moved to Elance) and wants you to be their first project on the new platform. Our experience is that you get what you pay for. Forget the lowest cost provider unless he or she has a high feedback score. You'll be glad you did.

Intellectual and Copyrights

Be sure that you spell out, either in the description of the project or in your independent contractor agreement you sign, that the work performed becomes yours exclusively and that all intellectual property rights and copyrights are assigned to you.

The project should always be "for hire" and you don't want to imply ownership, but spell it out directly and clearly before you get down to work. A lot of times the vendor will ask you if they can use it as a portfolio piece, which should be fine in most cases, so long as you're on the same page about who owns the work.

In the online resources section for this book you will find a contract template that can be modified and used for engaging contractors on sites like Elance.com. Simply specify the work being provided, specific deliverables and payment milestones, save it as a new document, and upload it to the workroom that will be created on Elance. com once you hire a contractor.

RULES OF THE ROAD
Best Practices for Your Lifestyle Entrepreneur Business

When it comes to building and deploying the necessary components of The Operations Model to support your Vision, there are several resources online that will save you time and money. Unless you already have the skills, it's far smarter to hire an expert to do some of the more specialized work, such as managing your AdWords campaigns or designing your logo. And even if you are an expert, you will still want to contract these things out so you can use your experience to provide direction, while being able to focus on other aspects of your business.

> *The secret to saving money when hiring service providers to operate parts of your business is to have an exact description of what you need to have done.*

Even if you're not an expert in design, copywriting, packaging, programming, etc. don't let the people you're considering know this. Just frame it as though you could effectively do the work yourself, but would rather save time by bringing in a professional contractor. This will put you in a stronger negotiating position for hiring top talent for the lowest possible cost.

Don't Pay Until You Really Need It

Any service you use should be free, low cost or pay-per-user. Many tools and services that are available on the Internet are available for free up to a certain level of usage. After you reach that point, you either sign up for the premium offer or you can pay as you go. Other times, there are tools that are available at no cost ever, such as Google Analytics. Another example is TeamBox.com which is an online collaboration platform for project management. You can create up to three projects for free, and then you can upgrade to keep adding more accounts for a small fee.

Service Level Agreements (SLA)

Agreements with service providers should be flexible and renewable. Ideally, you can cancel any agreement or let go of a contractor with no more than thirty days' notice if they are no longer needed or they simply aren't up to the task. It's always a good idea to enter into a trial period before creating the SLA. This protects you both from unnecessary contractual obligations. Like if you hire a sales person who was great at "selling you" on their abilities, but can't perform in the market where it really counts.

Service providers should agree to work through email addresses you provide. Every member of your team should appear as if they work for you. This means each of them should be willing to use email accounts routed through your domain, as in **ProvidersName@YourBusiness.com**. In doing so, all the email records are stored on your email services so you can access communications easily if there is a conflict. Also, it keeps the different parties from stealing any business from you by routing emails through their own email addresses.

Your expectations should be spelled out clearly and if something goes wrong you are responsible for enforcing the terms. Every project (website development, copywriting, customer service, etc.) should have specific milestones outlined at the beginning. If there are consequences for missing a deadline, these need to be spelled out as well. The goal is to stop the domino effect whereby a provider's failure to execute a task results in delays, thus causing other projects to fall behind and consequent revenue loss.

Designing a Memorable Logo

Describe the personality of your business in words. What is the perception that you want your customers to have? A high-end provider with a focus on customer service? A least-cost manufacturer who has lightning fast delivery times? A creative company with innovative products?

Give the prospective designer samples of other logos you like and tell them why. Also, provide them with a basic color scheme. You don't need to know the exact colors to use, but you should be able to say what colors you like and what ones you definitely do not like. If you want a tagline used with the logo, send some of your ideas along.

You may even want to provide a basic sketch of the logo, scanning a rough drawing into your computer and sending it along with the request for proposals. Just make sure you give your designer creative freedom to improve on your idea. Otherwise, you may be limiting your design options and not end up as happy as you could have been with your logo. Finally, remember that a logo has a long shelf life. So give it a lot of deliberation. Changing a logo can be difficult and expensive, as you want it to become instantly identifiable with your brand.

Website Design for the Lifestyle Entrepreneur

Building a quality website follows the same logic as designing a good logo. In fact, designing your logo should give you an idea of the color scheme, style and overall look of your website. After all, the logo defines your brand and the website is an extension and expansion of that brand.

Go on an online field trip and look at other sites. Copy down the URLs of sites you like and don't like. Tell the designer why you like them or don't like them. Don't be tempted to emulate the sites of your competitors. Look around outside your own industry for sites you like. While you don't want to copy your competitor's look and feel, you do want to see what stands out on their site and what looks out of place. This will give you a "best practices" model for your own website, knowing what works and what doesn't work on other sites.

It's OK to submit a rough sketch of what you want, or copy and paste together different pieces from other sites. For example, you may like the top of one, the navigation menu placement on another and the content section of a third. The more information you can give the designer, the less your site will cost to develop because it will greatly reduce the creative stage.

Copywriting

A great copywriter will save you an awful lot of time. As you know, it can be pretty hard to write about a subject that you're very close to. A professional copywriter can save you time and angst as you struggle to describe your products, services, company and brand. You don't need to have a copywriter who has experience in your industry. What you do want is a copywriter who knows how to do SEO writing while still selling.

Remember, your main goal of your website is to sell products and/or services. So the copy has to support that at every point, having the right balance between SEO and Sales. When selecting a writer, ask them for samples of other sites they've worked on. Supply them with the site's architecture you have in mind so they know how many pages and how much copy for each they will have to write. You'll also need some boilerplate copy for the Terms of Use and Privacy Policy pages. Make sure they can provide these.

SEO Provider

Hiring an SEO provider is easy compared to the creative fields of design and writing. Ask prospective vendors to give you a list of clients and the terms they rank highly for. Go to Google and see how they actually rank. Remember that it's far more impressive to be ranked 5th out of 30 million search results than to be 1st among 250,000 results.

It's not really important how every client has ranked, but you want to make sure that the provider is good with the big, high-value search terms. If they can rank highly for the competitive keywords, they should have no problem with your niche search terms. Providers generally want a minimum three- to four-month contract. This is standard, since it takes time for the search engines to index your site and for the provider to work their magic.

AdWords Campaign Management

Before you ever farm this function out, it's highly recommended that you do the first few yourself, so you can learn the process of building, refining and managing an AdWords campaign. The experience is invaluable and you'll learn a lot about how your customers find you. If you identify certain unexpected trends or discover new keyword combinations that convert well, you can adjust the meta tags and copy on your web pages accordingly to use those terms.

Generally you should structure compensation based on "leads received". Try to avoid any agreements where you end up paying a percentage of the total advertising budget. It's way too easy for a campaign team to simply run up your tab without having any leads to show for it. Alternatively, you can suggest a flat monthly fee, defining the budget and setting the baseline number of qualified leads expected, with incentives for outperforming the expectations.

YOUR VIRTUAL IT DEPARTMENT
Configuring Your Technologies & Infrastructure
Customer Relationship Management (CRM):

This is the most important component of your information technology setup. Think of it as the nerve center for all the operations of your business. It's here that you create Sales Orders and Invoices for customers, and where your fulfillment teams can publish information regarding production costs of your sales. Your CRM also serves as a database repository for all activity related to past and present orders. If you're building your business in order to sell it, a CRM will help support your asking price as you can point to your customer base and recurring business, and offer to transfer the CRM account as part of the sale.

You can set up a CRM system in a few ways. Sites like Alibaba.com have vendors in their Software section that have ready-made, easily customizable CRM solutions that are geared specifically for e-commerce of various goods. You can also hire programming firms from sites such as Elance.com or Guru.com to customize free open-source CRM software such as SugarCRM. Perhaps the easiest solution, however, is using off-the-shelf software-as-a-service (SaaS) CRM platforms such as Salesforce.com, crm.zoho.com, or vtiger.com.

My recommendation: Use Zoho.com to start with. It's free for up to three uses and very affordable thereafter. Their CRM setup already includes all the forms and modules you will need for your business (Sales Order, Invoice, Purchase Order, etc.).

If you want a full-featured, very robust solution, take a look at www.InfusionSoft. com - this is the top-of-the-line small business solution for e-commerce, CRM and email marketing, but it costs a few hundred dollars per month.

Interactive Voice Response System (IVR):

This is the face of your company, via telephone. Typically, a toll-free phone number on your website routes to your IVR system. It's here that your customers can be routed to appropriate departments and if the caller leaves a message, it will send emails with mp3 audio files of the call to your team members. Your IVR system can forward calls to any numbers in the world, allowing your team to be distributed across country or across the globe. A search in your country for "IVR providers" or "get toll-free number" will yield many options for you to choose from.

Suffice it to say that your initial system can be pretty basic, as long as it can forward calls to any numbers you designate. Also, you can sign up for SkypeIn numbers from Skype.com and route the IVR to your team members' SkypeIn numbers, which will ring on their computers if they are working, or on their phones if they are offline. This is especially cost effective if you are routing calls internationally, as it will cut out potentially costly long distance calling fees.

Having a toll-free number gives the outward appearance that you are a well-established company. But it doesn't have to cost much at all. Include your toll-free number on business cards and any marketing materials alongside your URL. The two work hand-in-hand to bring you new potential customers.

My recommendation: Use eVoice.com or Angel.com – They include a toll-free number when you create an account and the pricing is competitive. You can configure the IVR from your web browser and even have them professionally record a voice menu from text prompts that you provide. eVoice.com may still be offering six months free and a professionally recorded greeting when you sign up, which is only $9.95/mo. thereafter, and you can cancel anytime. Great way to sound like a total pro for literally no money.

File and Folder Sharing Solution:

It is essential that you be able to share files and collaborate with partners and providers no matter where you (or they) are in the world. To that extent, a file and folder sharing platform like www.Dropbox.com is a lifesaver. Using file and folder sharing solutions allow you to transmit information and large files efficiently and cost-effectively. Specifically, when you use Dropbox, you have a folder on your desktop, that is connected to a cloud-based website. You can share folders with other users at which point a copy of the folder appears on their desktop and both of you can work on files and transmit data without sending it via email.

As the business owner, you can set up a Dropbox folder with many sub-folders with names mirroring the components in The Operations Model. So, you could have a Sales folder, a SEO folder, an AdWords folder, etc., and then share each folder with the service providers or team members collaborating with you on that aspect of your business. This way the business flow becomes real-time; as soon as new files are added or modified, you are notified and can immediately check what has been done.

My recommendation: Set up a Dropbox.com account and structure your folder with sub-folders pertaining to each aspect of your business. Also set up a free account on www.YouSendIt.com. With these two accounts you can keep a real-time log of important files via Dropbox and have the option to send files up to 200mb via YouSendIt.

The best part? This is entirely Free! You can store up to 2gb of files in Dropbox before being asked to upgrade. Even then it's only $9.99/mo. YouSendIt is free for up to 200mb files and then you can subscribe to send files up to 2gb in size as well as select secure delivery options and more.

CONCLUSION

It's like I said at the start: If you take only 10% of the information in this book and put it into practice, it will change your life. From the Discover Your Identity exercise and designing Creative Constructs, to creating a Vision-MAP and building your Type of Lifestyle Entrepreneur business using The Operations Model, hopefully you found some useful information in here.

Writing and editing this book was a challenge in the sense that it could have easily been a 500 page book. I tried to condense much information down to its essence and convey the concepts in simple language with stories and illustrations for reference.

There are so many ways to take these ideas and apply them to life situations beyond even the scope of this book. What if you revisited the Discover Your Identity exercise and focused on a totally new interest or passion?

The possibilities really are endless when you let your mind go and try to imagine a lifestyle that reflects your most elaborate dreams. Acknowledging that desire, recognizing an ambition to improve the quality of your life is the starting point for all greatness. It is almost as if, once you draw a line in the sand and demand excellence from yourself, the universe can't help but accommodate you over time. Ambition + Persistence = Excellence!

> If you take only 10% of the information in this book and put it into practice, it will change your life.

It is true, now we have reached the end of this book, but truly, once you close this book, you should open a new chapter in your own life. Turn the page and move away from that which makes you unhappy and disillusioned. Move confidently toward the vision of your life that satisfies you and will bring joy and honor to those around you.

I always love hearing how readers take these ideas and apply them to their lives. If you have an inspirational story, a lingering question, or just feeling like dropping a line and saying "hi", please don't hesitate to write me:

Jesse@JesseKrieger.com

Finally, and perhaps most importantly, I would like to invite you to check out all the extra resources and bonus information contained on the book website. There you will find download-able versions of the exercises in this book so you can print them out and work on them as many times as you would like.

There you will also find a community of like-minded individuals and a blog where I'll regularly post updates, expand on the ideas in this book and share what I'm currently excited about and focusing on:

www.JesseKrieger.com

Even though we have now reached the end of this book, let this mark the beginning many new adventures you will have as a Lifestyle Entrepreneur!

Thanks for reading and here's to your success,

Jesse Krieger

Jesse Krieger

Join my signature virtual bootcamp: www.BusinessInAWeekend.co

Join the community at the blog: www.LifestyleEntrepreneurBlog.com

ABOUT THE AUTHOR

Jesse Krieger

Jesse Krieger was born and raised in San Francisco but spends 3-4 months a year traveling the world. From climbing volcanoes with friends in the Mediterranean to consulting with clients from Malaysia to Manhattan, Jesse views the world as both playground and potential addressable market.

During his twenties Jesse has started over five companies and managed to sell two of them. He has lived, worked and traveled to over 30 countries and speaks German and Mandarin Chinese in addition to his native English.

A graduate of UC Berkeley and formerly a touring rock guitarist, Jesse counts becoming a published author as his most recent achievement. When he is not consulting with clients on lifestyle design and entrepreneurship, he can usually be found on a bicycle, pedaling up a steep mountain slope or yelling at the top of his lungs from the peak.

JESSE KRIEGER PRESENTS

BECOME A LIFESTYLE ENTREPRENEUR

6-DISC AUDIO TRAINING PROGRAM

www.BecomeALifestyleEntrepreneur.com

Jumpstart your journey towards living a life of fun and fulfillment as a lifestyle entrepreneur with this in-depth audio training program! Available immediately as an online course, complete with membership portal and bonuses.

Disc 1: Become a Lifestyle Entrepreneur and Creating Your Vision-MAP

Disc 2: Discover Your Identity & How to Identify Your Market

Disc 3: The Right Type of Business For You – Turn Your Interests and Passions into Products and Services

Disc 4: Master The 21ˢᵗ Century Internet Economy

Disc 5: How to Build Websites, Drive Traffic and Promote Your Business Online

Disc 6: How to Succeed and Grow as a Lifestyle Entrepreneur and Why Some People Never Win

>> Now Only $97.00 <<
www.BecomeALifestyleEntrepreneur.com

LIFESTYLE ENTREPRENEURS ACADEMY PRESENTS

BUSINESS
IN A WEEKEND

www.BusinessInAWeekend.co
Ready to take your lifestyle and business to the next level?

Join best selling author Jesse Krieger and a community of like-minded lifestyle entrepreneurs on the Business In a Weekend virtual bootcamp and start building a business to finance the lifestyle of your dreams today!

The Business In a Weekend virtual bootcamp is run LIVE by Jesse Krieger via webinar, private Facebook group and membership portal so you can participate from anywhere in the world.

Business In a Weekend is:

Core Training – Seven 90-120 minute live webinar trainings covering everything from idea generation and building websites, to launching and growing your own online business.

Community – Access to a private Facebook group to get questions answered, feedback on your work and make new friends and business partnerships

Continuity – Lifetime access to an exclusive membership portal with exercises, downloadable PDFs, hiring scripts and all the training webinar recordings to watch any time.

SPECIAL READER BONUS: Get $200 off your ticket! Use code: **LifestyleReader200**

Go here and register for a free webinar: **www.BusinessInAWeekend.co**

Then register and use this promo code: **www.BusinessInAWeekend.co/join**

To your success,

Jesse Krieger
Author of Lifestyle Entrepreneur
Creator of Business In a Weekend

LIFESTYLE ENTREPRENEURS ACADEMY
MONTHLY MASTERMIND TRAINING

www.MonthlyMastermindTraining.com

*"More coaching, accountability and community
each month than most people get in a year."*

I invite you to join a community of like-minded lifestyle entrepreneurs and get coaching from me, Jesse Krieger, my friend and total marketing badass Konstantinos Kaloulis, and some of the most talented and successful coaches on earth.

The Monthly Mastermind Training program consists of:

Monthly Master Class Webinar with Jesse Krieger and Konstantinos Kaloulis with live Q&A that is recorded and transcribed.

Tactical Business Assets such as hiring scripts for web designers and programmers on Elance to save $$...or a profitable, high-converting Facebook ad campaign blueprint)

Facebook "Ask Us Anything" Sessions – Jesse and Konstantinos answer questions in the private Facebook group and facilitate introductions to other entrepreneurs that can help you crush it with your business.

Contest For Prizes - Put your newly learned skills to the test and win prizes like a new iPad or a deep-dive 1-to-1 coaching session with Jesse

Having the right coaches and access to the right resources helps entrepreneurs grow their businesses 350% faster than those who try to be a "one man army" and do it all themselves. Give yourself the gift of *crushing it* this year and join us in the Monthly Mastermind Training program!

SPECIAL READER BONUS: Get your first month of training for only $1.00!

Go here to apply for the program: **www.MonthlyMastermindTraining.com**

Then use this code with your application: **LifestyleMastermind1**

To your success,

Jesse Krieger

Author of Lifestyle Entrepreneur

Co-Creator of Monthly Mastermind Training